Fancy That!

Fancy That!

J M Fancy

Copyright © 2023 by J M Fancy

All rights reserved. No part of this book may be reproduced or used in any manner without written permission of the copyright owner except for the use of quotations in a book review.

This book is purely for entertainment only and not a substitute for professional services. Should you need to seek professional advice, please do so from a relevant qualified expert.

FIRST EDITION

ISBNs
Paperback: 978-1-80227-900-9
Hardcover: 978-1-80541-085-0
eBook: 978-1-80227-901-6

Dedication

I could not have written this book without my dear departed Mother, Doreen. I will always remember the day, sharing some wine on a late summer afternoon. The book always started with the Morphing men, but the first pages were created with the flying shit; how we both laughed. At least you got to read my manuscript Mum, but unfortunately never got to hold my book. I know you will be looking down, along with my dear Dad, Peter, and my Grandmother, Emma; you are all missed so dearly.

I wish to thank my dear friends who believed in me, they know who they are.

A big thank you to A4, without him the world would not have known our story.

Thank you to my beautiful daughter "London" for pushing me to complete "Fancy That!" (Even though she raised a few eyebrows along the way) and still does.

And blessings to my grandchildren, that they may, upon reaching 18, laugh and say, what the hell was nanny writing about!

A big thank you to my first editor, Kim Kimber, without you piecing this all together, I could never have progressed.

And lastly, this song is for you, A4. After all, we both love Ella.

I could write a book...and I just have!

('I Could Write a Book', Ella Fitzgerald, *GOLD*, 2005.)

Contents

Chapter 1 Morphing Men.................. 1

Chapter 2 The journey begins 7
To love or to be in love 10

Chapter 3 My American Boy...........17
A4's arrival.......................................22
Did you know (sex in water) 30
Did you know (Lizards)................. 34
Article St Petes Times
Tampa USA......................................44

Chapter 4 Back to my flight 51
Perfect stimulation.........................52
Back at the airport..........................56
Couples that stay together 64

Chapter 5 Fun in the sky 69
   Toilet brigade 72
   Flying shit! 73
   Arctic Narwhal! 74
   The Pussy Wink 78
   Dough! 81
   Mr Latino 84

Chapter 6 Tango or Tantric sex 87
   Farting and Flatulence................. 90
   Did you know (Vaginal farts) 92
   Mr Funny 93
   Let's get sexy 98

Chapter 7 So let's explore frisson....101
   Mr Lover 104
   Did you know (A whales blowhole) 110
   Mr Spa 111
   The Nymphy handshake 114

Contents

Chapter 8   Our descent 117
   Mr DIY 121
   Room 1 – The Ice bedroom suite...126
   Room 2: Numinous encounter 127
   Did you know (people you
   know and past life's)....................129
   Room 3: Santa's North Pole
   rocket ride.....................................131
   Did you know (Blue Lotus)...........135

Chapter 9   Santa's farewell gifts ...139
   My chocolate box of Morphs 140
   Did you know (chocolate) 143

Chapter 10 The conference.............145
   Spiritual philosophy.....................145
   Psychic sex, Telepathy:
   awakening our sexual
   spiritual mind...............................156

Something I am proud of.

I am proud to have come this far and written my first book. Having been taught English using the Initial Teaching Alphabet (ITA) as a young child, in the 1960s/1970s, for me, this is a huge achievement.

Many of today's generation of teachers will never even have heard of ITA because it was discontinued in mainstream school years ago. I have always wanted to write a book, but the ITA nonsense squashed my confidence. However, I have managed to overcome these early difficulties, otherwise you would not be reading this.

Chapter 1

Morphing Men

"They could all be kept in a little box and selected when desired."
Let me explain.

Some years ago, I recall sitting in my office exchanging banter with my female work colleagues. All of them were moaning about their partners:

- 'He doesn't listen, and he never takes the bins out.'
- 'He doesn't understand me.'
- 'He just wants a quickie; our romance has died.'

- 'He never makes me laugh anymore.'
- 'If we go away, I organise everything, even down to packing his suitcase.'
- 'After years of making packed lunches for the kids, I still get up early to make his sandwiches.'
- 'He can't even put down the shower mat. There's a strong chance of me slipping and breaking my neck on the wet floor.'
- 'I have to inspect the toilet for clues just in case I get a floaty surprise.'

So, I immediately asked them, 'What do you want from a relationship?'

- 'Don't your partners feel the same way about you?'
- 'It's just not women who moan; surely men do it to?'

They seemed to ignore my last two questions and jumped on board to answer the first. In no particular order, they each reached out and provided me with the following:

- 'Companionship,' one of them confirmed! 'Someone who shares rather than takes.'
- 'Laughter, someone to laugh with.'
- 'For him to support my career,' another one replied. 'It's all about his career.'
- 'For him to celebrate my achievements. He never tells me, "Well done".'
- 'Someone to make me a packed lunch.'
- 'A man who recognises, after years of bringing up his children, that I am not his Cinderella.'
- 'Someone who has time for sex, real intimate sex, like we had in the beginning, and without his socks on.'
- 'For him to make a lot more effort with my friends and family. It feels like he hates spending time with them.'
- 'Massages without sex for once.'

I sat there for a while, before interrupting their debate. They were all now speaking over each other. 'Hey, ladies, so he wakes up thinking of sex. You wake up thinking...'

- 'What can I cook for dinner tonight?'
- 'Has Zachary got money for his school trip to Europe?'
- 'Have I booked Xenia's birthday party?'
- 'I need to send back that dress I ordered because it's too small (having gained weight because I never have enough time to go to a slimming club, let alone the time or money for a gym).'

They all replied, 'Exactly!'

I smiled and thought about this further. Hmm!

It seems a high percentage of couples turn their partners into a carer. I mean, most men love a confident woman but, unfortunately, many women turn into confident sandwich makers.

I strive to remember my own marriage vows. Maybe I should have added, something like this: 'Till death us do part, in sickness and in health, and to be a talented sandwich maker'.

I would then have been able to use the following phrase: 'Would you like cheese, egg or a fucking kick up the arse in your sandwich, my love, huh?'

As I continued to listen to my colleagues' displeasure with their relationships, I had this cool idea of 'Morphing Men'.

How delightful it would be if the men we all secretly wished for 'happened' to have their own individual skills to give to you, just when you required them:

- You need your bedroom decorated, out morphs 'Mr DIY'.
- You need great sex, out morphs 'Mr Lover'.
- You really need a laugh, out morphs 'Mr Funny'.
- You want to dance, out morphs 'Mr Latino'.
- You desire a massage without nonsense, out morphs 'Mr Spa'.

- You really want someone easy on the eye, out morphs 'Mr Good-Looking'.
- You are hungry, out morphs 'Mr Michelin Chef'.
- You need money, out morphs 'Mr Rich'.
- You desire an affair, out morphs 'Mr Overseas'.

Maybe they could all be kept in a little box and selected when desired.

Chapter **2**

The journey begins

I was on my way to chair a conference and give a speech on spiritual philosophy. Sitting in the departure lounge, waiting for my flight to be called, I started to observe people around me. I glimpsed a couple caressing one another (caressing was an understatement). They were seated to my far left but I had spotted them. I knew the signs. The couple couldn't keep their hands off one another. For God's sake! This was immensely embarrassing. If only they would leave each other alone; it seemed they had 'Just Met'!

I had been seated for some time now and I was becoming uncomfortable. My back ached, and my bottom had started to stick to the black, faux-leather plastic, perched on a tube of four metal legs. You know what I mean? It's about time someone came up with a more comfortable form of seating in airports. Why do the seats need to be attached? It's like passengers are lined up for a criminal identification parade.

As I wriggled about, adjusting my bottom, my attention returned to 'Mr and Mrs Just Met'. My eyes looked through them, as I remembered back to a time when I had experienced the same thing.

Yes, I had also been like an octopus on heat. However, this stage, of continually kissing and caressing one another, had lasted approximately six months. But it was exciting at the time, and oh so memorable. You too, have probably experienced what it feels like to be in a new, exciting, consensual relationship.

The journey begins

What's wrong with us all? No, really. It seems attraction only lasts for a short spell. Many label this as 'lust', while others refer to it as 'passion'. When this phase ends, we seem fixated on pushing away someone whom we so lovingly and exclusively aspired to be with. Is this where it starts and ends: the passion fails to retain its appeal, the boredom in the bedroom sets in and we desire 'secret sex'? An affair!

Wanderlust is awakened once more. We cheat. We want secret sex, but why? Because it's amazingly different. More importantly, it's short-lived because once that secret thing has subsided and it's no longer secret, it is no longer desired. That longing, that desire for something different, once again, becomes 'boring'. It goes full circle and has run its course. You may have discovered this yourself or been on the receiving end, or you may have been tempted, but the forbidden fruit was too much for you to handle. Maybe your hidden secret may have been revealed. ('Secret Love', Georgie B & Deborah Bell, *Luxury Soul*, 2018.)

To love or to be in love

Everyone who falls in love expects it to last forever, but the sad truth is that relationships unavoidably change, people change, and we seek new adventures. This doesn't happen to everyone; some people make it. They remain together through thick and thin. That's because they 'shift' and want to do so. They do not need 'Morphing Men'. Well, OK, maybe they would secretly like them!

A big 'high five' to you all; the millions that stay together. But many, who are not so privileged, don't unfortunately. Sadly, communication between partners seems to break down and this threatens the relationship. You both want different things, you have grown and your need for your partner is no longer required, desired, or expected.

The journey begins

What happened to the love that first drew you both together? That magical, mystical surge that awakens your soul. That time when you cannot eat or sleep, weight seems to fall off you effortlessly and your spirit seems to be awakened and nourished by the mystery and meaning of being in love. Or is this feeling not love at all? Is to be in love just lust? It's a fact that you can never get this feeling back. Once it's gone and run its course, it's gone, period. That's because we shift; we no longer feel the need to keep touching the goods (your partner).

You may have been mesmerised by the highest form of enlightenment that comes from unconditional love via the universe. However, you must differentiate or, more appropriately, distinguish, the difference between 'being in love' and loving someone. Once you ascertain this and identify the differences, you can then make choices.

Being 'in love' and loving someone may feel the same but they are hugely different. It doesn't matter what age you are; it is imperative you know and understand the difference. I think this is where so many of us fall down.

To be 'in love' is lust. It's a form of possessiveness and obsession with an individual. Another word for it is 'infatuation', and this can lead to 'narcissistic behaviour' but that's another subject, taboo for now, which we will explore later.

You 'love' your partner, parents, children, friends or pet. You love them, unconditionally, through thick or thin. You love them, without possessiveness and want to take care of them, no matter what.

Maybe, that's why the older couple, 'Mr & Mrs Duty-Free', to whom you will be introduced to shortly, and, of course, 'Mr & Mrs Just Met', are all in the moment. They know what it is to 'love' someone. They have passed the 'being in love' stage and/or they can't get enough of each other.

'Mr & Mrs Just Met' are in the 'being in love' store and have not got all their groceries yet. They still need to go shopping. Wink! Their desire to keep touching the 'goods' simply amplifies tenfold. It's all new to them and they can't get enough of each other. It's like being introduced to the latest tasty chocolate biscuit or savoury cracker, but after a time you get bored because you have eaten so many - then, out of the blue, comes a tasty lemon cheesecake or a delicious chocolate sponge.

> ***'From the moment one has obtained something desired, it is no longer desirable. The desire to obtain something disappears at the moment it is obtained.'***
> ***~ Kama Sutra***

So, this is the reason you fancy lemon cheesecake until it no longer serves you; of course, you now fancy a cracker, cheese and maybe some onion.

Many relationships are in that crossover period, they are somewhere in between 'being in love' and loving someone. It's like standing in the middle of the bridge - you started out at one end but need to reach the other side. They both need to work out if they will ride the storm or release one another.

When you can identify what stage you are in, being 'in love' or loving, and come to terms with it, realising there will be a change, a shift, only then can you make choices about your desires and needs. Fundamentally, you can then question your partner. Do you both want the same things? Will he/she get upset if you don't give them a nightly blow job? Will you get upset when he/she doesn't rub your feet any more or no longer makes love to you like they did at the beginning of the relationship?

If not, go to see a marriage counsellor, run like the wind, or realise you have 'shifted'. So, have you shifted to remain with your partner or shifted on to a whole new path, alone and waiting for your next adventure? ('I Need You for Your Love!', Kim Tibbs, *Luxury Soul*, 2017.)

Chapter 3

My American Boy

Let me tell you about a snippet of unexpected love that I, myself, experienced. This is a true story!

Many years ago, coffee in hand, my friend and I started to search an online dating site for men (not for me, I was going through a divorce). I was helping my friend, of course. Well, that is what I had envisioned.

We decided to change it up a little and search across the pond (the Big Apple), New York City, USA. We were both resident in London, UK. However, it was not my friend who found a potential partner, but me.

Suddenly, this guy stared back at me from his profile picture; everything about him was 'me'. We had the same taste in music, he loved to cook and travel. We shared a love of jazz, especially Ella Fitzgerald and Sarah Vaughan. Even both our parents loved this kind of music. My mother and father had taken me, as a child, to see Ella Fitzgerald at the Royal Festival Hall, in London, UK, in 1975, and she went on to feature at Ronnie Scott's, one of the world's most famous jazz clubs in London. I had not been that impressed back then, but now, as an adult, I appreciate being able to witness such a performance at an early age. I had been exposed to something wonderful and I am so profoundly grateful to my parents.

Going back to what me and this guy had in common, the list was endless, it was like everything about him was a duplicate of me. Was he my soul mate? Do soul mates really exist?

Before I knew it, my friend had printed off a copy of his profile from the website, onto a piece of white, A4 paper, which I placed on my front passenger seat. However, I never expected in a million years that a few months later he would manifest in person and accompany me in the front seat of my little car. Upon arriving home, after visiting my friend, I placed his A4 profile in my kitchen. I never imagined what followed would be so wonderful. (By the way, the most common paper size, in the UK, is A4, used for printing and stationery).

Days went by, until temptation set in. I eventually mustered up the courage to send him an email. By the way, to send an email back in those days was not as simple as it is now. You had to dial up via the phone line; a modem (what a performance that was). I can still hear the annoying ring tone as I dialled up.

Scratching my head, hoping for inspiration about what to write, I managed to put together the following: 'Hi, how are you? What's it like in the USA?' I know you are probably thinking pathetic, right? But it worked.

After a few sleepless nights of 'what did you do that for?' and the total humiliation of rejection (no one likes rejection, huh?) he replied. What a result; yippee! he had acknowledged me from across the pond.

He, A4, had asked by email if he could 'place the first call'. I was intrigued by him asking if he could 'place' the first call. Not being accustomed to the American way of speaking, 'place' was somewhat alien to me. Hmm, okay. You can 'place'. From the first of many long telephone calls, to hear his voice was extraordinary. My voice appeared to captivate him, also. It was like he had pulled me towards him with a big lasso, hoping to capture me. After all, he was from North America. A4 was trying to pull me across that big blue ocean with his long rope and, in one of his subsequent emails he, my American boy, did just that. He spoke of his lasso.

After a few exchanged emails and somewhat long 'placed' evening phone calls, it seemed fate took over and my amore was destined for the United Kingdom. I will never forget that one, oh so memorable, email.

A4's email instructed me to 'scroll down' and scrolling down, led me to the following:

- Flight No: BA 5104
- Destination London Heathrow
- Summer 2003

I was so shocked. I felt like a child. My heart raced with excitement and an anxious feeling swirled around my body.

My lover, A4, *mi amore*, was of American/Italian descent and 6 feet 3 inches tall. He told me he had never been to London before, and certainly not to Italy, although his grandmother originated from Venice. Without hesitation, we both agreed to visit Venice during his short stay in the UK, and we did. Practically within twenty-four hours of him arriving in the UK, we had flown to Venice and touched down at Treviso airport. ('Quando, Quando, Quando', Michael Bublé – with Nelly Furtado, *It's Time* 2005.)

A4's arrival

At London Heathrow Airport, I anxiously waited for A4's flight to arrive from New Jersey, USA. With my heart pounding, I waited in arrivals and listened for an American accent, and there it was...people started to come through speaking with a distinctive American twang. My heart started to beat faster, and then he appeared. We had only ever spoken over the phone and via the internet. There was no skype back then. I must heed, I had taken serious precautions beforehand, meaning I did not meet up with a stranger I knew nothing about. I had met his daughter and family via long distant phone calls and would encourage anyone in a similar situation to do the same.

As he walked through duty-free, heading towards the barriers where I was patiently waiting, I spotted all 6 feet 3 inches of him. He held a red rose in one hand and a beautiful picture of Venice in the other. My most abiding memory is of how tall he was and the smell of the black leather jacket he was wearing. As we locked eyes, both blushing for a moment, we embraced one another. We were like 'Mr & Mrs Just Met'.

A4 was inquisitive by nature. He was amazed at the many terraced houses in London, with their Mary Poppins' chimney pots. He loved London and would often go out to explore it via the Tube and buses.

Our first night together was magical. With the Stylistics playing in the background (Betcha By Golly Wow), positioned on the sofa, he introduced me to what he called 'his big guy'. Was this another North American saying? I really couldn't care less. The big guy was standing to attention, ready for action, but oh so silky smooth. Why is a penis so smooth? Maybe they are thickened silkworms under cover.

The next morning, we flew to Venice from London Stansted Airport. Upon arrival, we did the whole 'gondola' thing, and enjoyed a meal of lobster and crab by candlelight *al fresco* while the gondolas danced in the moonlight, bobbing on the banks of the Grand Canal. And oh, we kissed in St Mark's Square and admired the view from the bell tower. All within twenty-four hours!

I can still picture and smell his damp, muscular body as he towel-dried his skin after a shower in our hotel room. A4 was standing in front of me. Our room was somewhat dimly lit, and the low lighting reflected his white towel, which was perfectly placed around his hips. He then sprayed his torso with 'Curve' eau de cologne by Liz Claiborne;

the aromatic green fragrance for men. This was my American boy's signature scent; it captured my heart and has hypnotised my soul for all eternity.

To this very day, if I catch a hint of 'Curve', I am swept back to 2003, Venice and the Bauer Hotel. Maybe you have a scent of your own that transports you back to your lover, your own memories.

After finishing our meal from our hotel's own "De Pisis restaurant", and returning to our room, temptation took over me. Playing mellow background music, I started to dance for him. I danced with the iron in our room, his tie, and whatever else I could get my hands on.

My American stallion was mesmerised; it was like I had put him in a hypnotic state of pleasure. I can still see his shy, seductive facial expression as he watched me. He lay in bed, nestling against the crisp, white pillows, propped against the wooden headboard. His dark brown hair was swept back as he spread his perfectly manicured fingers over his forehead and into his hairline. He looked youthful, as he watched me through soulful eyes.

So why dance with an iron you might ask? Who knows, pole dancing was not a thing back in those days. Well, maybe that's wrong. For sure, there was no pole in our bedroom, but hey. Let's get clarity on this. There was no pole in our bedroom, only his 'big guy' standing to attention.

Never did I imagine, several months down the line, we would be skinny dipping in CocoCay via Royal Caribbean; my 40th birthday present from A4.

I had never been on a cruise before. I flew from the UK to Tampa, Florida, to stay with him and then depart on the short cruise. I recall having to complete a document before we embarked, so we stopped off at Cracker Barrel Old Country Store for a bite to eat and complete the form. It was quite straightforward, just asking me my name, date of birth, etc. However, being quite a confident woman, I could not understand why my hand had started to shake, was it nerves? I tried to cover it up, suggesting he went to the bathroom. Even to this day, I have never spoken to him about why, suddenly, I could not write without shaking. Sometimes nerves get the better of you and come on when you least expect it. Thank God my nerves never got the better of me when skinny dipping at CocoCay - quite the opposite. What a beautiful day that was.

We departed our cruise liner and jumped on board a tender boat which transported us to the private island of CocoCay, in the Bahamas, fifty-five miles north of Nassau. CocoCay is one of the Berry Islands; in fact, it was previously called 'Little Stirrup Cay'. With beach bag and sun lotion in hand, we managed to secure a couple of white sun loungers and, of course, opened a bottle or two of alcohol. I sipped on my favourite aperitif, Pernod and water, and A4 poured himself a glass of cabernet sauvignon. One would say an aperitif is an alcoholic drink taken before a meal to stimulate the appetite, but it seemed to stimulate something else! We left our sun loungers and headed off along the beach to a more remote area away from our fellow passengers.

I recall running through a colony of seagulls to enable access further down the beach. We eventually came across a large rock peeking out over the seashore. The sand on the island was incredibly white and extremely soft to walk on barefoot. The sea was turquoise, warm, and so inviting. The sky was totally blue, with no sign of a cloud.

A4 took my hand and said, 'Shall we skinny dip?'

Before I knew it, my pink bikini was off, and he didn't waste much time, either. He too, had stripped butt naked.

We swum together, enjoying the fun of not being able to have intercourse in the sea. Well, you could but with just water, there was no lubrication. We laughed and found the experience funny but that was short-lived as a large stingray headed our way. I immediately ran out of the water in a panic. When the danger had passed, we ventured back into the water, laying naked together, bobbing up and down as small waves lapped against us. Just as A4 was serving me, suddenly, from out of nowhere, appeared some of our fellow cruise passengers, kayaking! One after the other, there must have been six kayaks, paddling towards us, raising their paddles as if to give the thumbs up and shouting 'whoop whoop'! From what I recall they were women kayakers, who happened to catch another woman being sexually pleased.

A4 immediately jumped on top of me to cover my naked body. One of his best friends stated that the kayaking boats must have thought A4's bottom was where they should moor the kayaks, between the cheeks of his backside! That was certainly a wonderful memory, we were surely in love and were nowhere near the 'shift'. We had more intimate memories to make, and we did.

Did you know (sex in water)

To fully enjoy fantastic sex in water, you should insert silicon-based lubricant into the vagina beforehand, as water washes away your natural lubrication. If you reach an orgasm in the water, the vaginal contractions (the 'pussy wink', as I like to call it) create a sucking effect and can draw up water inside you and, if there is something lurking in the water, or maybe hot tub chemicals, it can cause a urine infection. Even though it makes sense to lubricate to enjoy ocean sex on the spur of the moment, we do not carry lubricant around with us. But, hey, maybe we should? The next time you go shopping for vacation toiletries, don't just pick up factor 20 sun lotion, mosquito repellent and anti-diarrhoea tablets: you better buy some lubricant and insert it before you apply the sun cream. You never know, you might get lucky!

Once we had disembarked from the cruise ship, we headed to lunch at Jack Willie's Bar, Grill & Tiki, in Oldsmar, Florida. The sun was shining, and it was extremely hot. We were seated at a table on two bar stalls, overlooking a small river. As we ordered a variety of food, I had no idea what A4 was about to do next. Just as our food arrived, he proposed to me. I couldn't believe it when he presented me with a stunning, princess cut diamond ring. I had never imagined, in a few days' time, I would be getting on that big British Airways Boeing with a ring on my finger, heading back to the UK. After all, I was on vacation and had to return home but, just in case you are wondering, I said yes to A4's marriage proposal. Absolutely, without any hesitation.

My point is this; magic can happen, and lust can turn into love. Most relationships comprise of around six months of lust and sex, before moving on in one way or another. Therefore, when I describe 'Mr & Mrs Just Met', you know I am referring to the initial phase of a relationship.

So, did me and my American boy get past that initial stage? Yes, we did. We got married and I took his name. After arriving in the USA on a fiancée visa, I married him at the Columbia Restaurant (Florida's oldest Restaurant and the largest Spanish restaurant in the world) on 7th Avenue, in Ybor City. (I mean, if it was good enough for Marilyn Monroe and the many stars that continue to visit, then it was good enough for us.) Our ceremony and wedding breakfast took place in the King's Room. We had Spanish cuisine, including black beans and rice, and enjoyed the Columbia's famous, signature '1905' salad. We even had traditional flamenco dancers twirling around in deep sky-blue dresses.

We were happy for a long while. The sad part was, after living in Florida for three years, I missed the UK and my family and friends. Like they say, you can take the girl out of London, but you can't take London out of the girl. I eventually returned my green card and went through the exit door, back to the UK.

People still ask me if I miss Florida. Well, yes, it's beautiful; it has stunning beaches and places of interest, and I miss the friends I made and our lovey home. I don't miss the alligators, lizards and snakes! Unless you are a true reptile lover, who would?

But, I do recall one evening, in particular, when the news reader had announced heavy rain and strong winds. Acting in haste, I instructed A4, with my help, to carry in the large metal BBQ and place it just inside our kitchen. Big mistake! But I was so worried the wind might lift the BBQ and smash it against the glass doors that looked out over our pool.

Our home was a bungalow, there were no stairs, so when we woke up in the morning, and entered the open plan kitchen/lounge, there they were - bloody loads of them all over the kitchen counter tops and lounge. Our home had been invaded by lizards that had been dormant in the BBQ, hiding from the sun's ray. They had all escaped the BBQ and had now taken over our home. Then they started doing that neck thing - 'throat puffing'!

I screamed and yelled at A4; this was a nightmare. It took ages to chase them all out of the bungalow and, days later, I would still jump when one appeared from the laundry basket or pantry. It certainly taught me a lesson: never bring your BBQ indoors, you don't know what might be lurking in there.

Did you know (Lizards)

Lizards, puff their throats out for a few reasons: as a defence of territory, when threatened and simply to attract a mate. Can you imagine a guy you fancy, doing that to you? Puffing out his throat, as much as to say, 'Come here, baby, let's get it on!' I know we aren't lizards, but I just hate it when they do the neck thing.

So, was there anything else I missed about Florida? Hmm!

I can say, with hand on heart, I do not miss those school kids, driving up my arse on a state road and I sure don't miss the hurricanes and downpours of rain.

Talking of downpours, on one occasion, I had just left my father-in-law's home in Holiday (yes, that really is the name - it's a suburb of Tampa), where he lived. It was a thirty-minute drive home from there and – stupid me - I drove into a horrendous storm. I could see the dark sky ahead, but I kept going.

The windscreen wipers couldn't keep up with the downfall of water pounding down on State Road 54. I felt like Dorothy from *The Wizard of Oz* entering a tornado. However, it wasn't a tornado but an overly aggressive storm. Visibility was extremely poor as I drove at five miles an hour following the taillights of a small, white van. To be honest, I don't know how I managed to stay on the road and not end up in a ditch with an alligator!

It eventually got lighter, the rain eased, and I could just about see the exit to home. That was one very scary drive indeed.

Going back to my memories of Florida, I do, absolutely miss the snow crab legs, served with garlic butter and, of course, a large cold beer. Buffalo, hot, chicken wings, blue cheese dip and celery are also missed. Obviously, eating these in the sunshine state is essential, especially at Hooters and the Crab Shack, both in Hudson Florida. The 'she-crab soup' is amazing, too, served at Scully's Waterfront Restaurant, Madeira Beach, near John's Pass Village, St Petersburg, Florida. I also miss the great Cuban sandwich, something my daughter would vouch for. In fact, her love of a Cuban pressed sandwich originated from Larry's Deli & Sandwich Shop, Land O' Lakes, Tampa. She made up her own selection being - turkey, American cheddar, lettuce, mayonnaise, and garlic pressed.

My daughter's American friends, from the local high school she attended, nicknamed her 'London'. My memory of her first day in an American high school was the yellow dungarees she wore and her perfect brunette hair she had straightened, without imperfections. I remember the many friends she made during our time in America, and, to this day, she still has in her life. Florida was absolutely life-changing for us all, but my daughter's story is for her to tell. I am sure, she may reveal all in her own memoirs, one day, to pass down to her children. 'London' is beautiful, and I am proud to be her Mum.

So, were there any more children in the marriage to A4? Yes, A4 had a daughter from a previous marriage, just like me. A4's daughter is beautiful, just like mine. They are very respectful of each other. A4 and I never had children together, but we were lucky to have two beautiful, intelligent daughters who became sisters...of a kind.

Going back to my memories, thinking about it, the funniest memory I have of Florida was when I worked for an exceptional chiropractor known to me as Dr Dom. I was employed as a massage therapist to assist patients before their chiropractic adjustments. The clinic was situated close to a nudist resort.

The Doctor advised me how he needed to promote his business. It was that time of the year when the snowbirds come down, it was winter in Florida, but the temperature was still hot. I had never seen a snowbird: why would snowbirds want to fly into a nudist resort?

The doctor chuckled as he explained 'snowbird' was a term used in Florida. A snowbird was a person who lived in a cold state of America and would fly down to Florida in the winter as the temperature was much warmer. Some snowbirds liked to stay in the nudist resorts. Well, that told me. Fancy that!

One extremely hot Saturday afternoon, the doctor, and I ventured out to the nudist resort I had agreed to attend with him. However, this was to promote his business while a volleyball tournament took place. Wearing my royal blue scrubs, we packed up the doctor's van with massage beds and off we went to visit some snowbirds. As we entered the large gates to the nudist camp, I couldn't believe my eyes. My first glimpse was of a naked man, riding a bicycle. He was around sixty years old with a large belly, and he was naked except for a straw hat, socks, and sandals. He was very tanned.

As he pedalled his bicycle in front of us, I looked at the doctor and let out a large belly laugh. I had never been subjected to anything like this before. The sight of this nudist man was alien to me. I ended up having a fit of nervous laughter.

We eventually pulled up on the grass and straight in front of us was the volleyball tournament. We put up our tent and massage tables. Everyone, apart from me and the doctor, was butt naked. I hid my shyness, behind my sunglasses.

Suddenly, I was approached by one of the doctor's patients. He walked towards me wearing a long white T-shirt that promoted his somewhat erect penis. He also wore a straw hat and sandals, but without socks.

After a brief conversation of pleasantries, the patient returned to the volleyball match.

I could see the swinging balls in the distance, and I don't mean the volleyballs! Breasts, penises, and balls hung high and low, as the nudists continued with their tournament but, oh no, the doctor's patient had returned. I think he was trying to ease me in with his white T-shirt, because now the T-shirt had gone, and the only thing left on his body was the straw hat and brown sandals. Thank God I still had my sunglasses on. I was so embarrassed and didn't know where to look but, naturally, my eyes went down to his big guy that looked conditioned in sun cream.

I had never encountered a nudist before but felt somewhat privileged to have done so. There are many nudists and, to be honest, each to their own. This was an experience and certainly an eye-opener. It must be a great feeling to expose your body like that, letting all your inhibitions go in front of people, but for me, I prefer some form of swimsuit worn in the sun. I think it's more sensual on the eye and promotes naughty thoughts of what's underneath.

The only thing I can add is this: by the time the doctor and I had finished, packed up and returned home, I had a severe headache from the sun and overwhelming sights I had witnessed. I lay down on our sofa and poured myself a large glass of red wine. After all, it's not every day your boss escorts you to a nudist resort. Thanks, Doctor Dom. That was certainly one fancy treat for me!

Going back to A4, I think our marriage failed due to the pull of two countries and the day A4 started his master's degree. We were incredibly happy, but a few months down the line, A4 announced he wanted to study for a master's degree. This had a detrimental effect on our relationship. A4 was working exceptionally long hours and weekends were mostly spent with him studying, which eventually led to a decline in our relationship. I felt like I wasn't getting the attention I deserved. A4 was tired, burnt out and I was getting more and more frustrated. I never imagined I would be spending so much time alone in an alien country.

I started smoking and, while A4 slept, I would secretly go into one of the bedrooms, puffing the smoke out onto the pool area. I would then take a shower, hoping A4 wouldn't smell the smoke on me. Time went by and, once again, I felt like Dorothy. I just wanted the ruby slippers to take me home to the UK.

Knowing I was unhappy, A4 agreed to accompany me on my return to the UK. We packed up our beautiful house and A4 secured a great job in Canary Wharf, London, but even though his working hours were shorter than in the US, he was miserable. The master's degree and work were really pulling him down. He now missed the US and, of course, his daughter. He booked a flight back to the States, leaving me in England.

We both felt empty, lost and without hope for our future together. We spoke every day on the phone, but the weeks and months went by where I could no longer handle being estranged from my husband. It had come to an end, and I asked for a divorce, which A4 was against.

I still believe the countries divided us. It's not that we didn't love each other. We just couldn't settle in each other's native land, and A4 studying for a master's degree dealt the final blow; it killed us.

We were both heartbroken, but we were lucky to experience the times we spent together, and I am profoundly grateful for the experience. We remain friends, but not friends with benefits. Wink!

A4 has since remarried and is happy. I can only wish them my best. He is real; come on, we got married and although the marriage ended, our memories are solid and delightful. In fact, we even made news on our wedding day in the *St. Petersburg Times*, Tampa, Florida.

Article St Petes Times Tampa USA

> ***St Petersburg Times, late Tampa edition***
>
> **'Ybor seals love story that bridged the Atlantic', April 19th, 2005**

Extracts from the article:

- 'I drove up and down 7th Avenue on a Sunday night, hoping to find something worthy to write about.'
- 'Even The Columbia appeared to be on the back end of a busy night, but when I peered into the restaurant's bar, my search ended, I saw my story.
- 'As the bartenders cleaned up, a bride and groom sat quietly, sipping wine.
- 'I didn't go looking for a love story, but I was thrilled to find one.'

Did you know?

I will let you into a little secret - well it is not a secret per se, but something that absolutely delighted me. Upon writing this book, and proud of the newspaper article Ernest Hooper wrote about us, I had a thought, and wondered if I went in search of him, would he remember me and A4. Much to my amazement, I found him, communicated with him and he was just as delighted I had made contact. He always wondered what the outcome was for us. Funny how things work out, and then, the craziest thing occurred to me, I had coincidently contacted him on April 19th, 2020, exactly fourteen years to the day our wedding article was posted in the *St Petersburg Times*. He called it serendipity, all over again! Ernest advised me that our story remains one of his favourites from his many years as a reporter/columnist. Truly an amazing guy.

Thank you, Ernest Hooper, for venturing out that evening in Ybor City, 2005, to the Columbia Restaurant and including us in your column. ('My One and Only Love', John Coltrane & Johnny Hartman, 1963.) This was our wedding song!

While writing this book, I approached A4 and asked him if he had a favourite memory of our time together. His first response was one of making meatloaf with me in the UK.

I felt somewhat deflated. Meatloaf! Was that it?

He wrote: 'First the meatloaf: The main thing was the meat, which was 50% ground lamb and 50% ground chicken. The spices were a typical Indian blend (onions, garlic, fresh cilantro, garam masala, cumin, turmeric, etc). Now I feel like making it. Memory coming!'

A4 then said he would think about this a bit more and come back to me. Two days later, he responded with this: 'My favourite memory doesn't concern a single event. It was the simple and routine act of being greeted by you after each long day of work and travel. The door would open, and there you would be; with cheeriness, a sweet voice, a 'Hi, darling' and lips puckered, ready for a delicate kiss. It was something I looked forward to each day, something I had never had, and something – particularly from you – that I greatly needed. There was closeness, love, care, and beauty every time the door opened.'

Fancy That!

Well, how beautiful was that and, hey, fancy that! A4 had presented me with more than I had expected and, as I read this, a song popped into my head! It mentions a delicate kiss, actually, 'when we kiss' and A4 had just revealed his memory of our own delicate kiss. (Lullaby of Birdland, Sarah Vaughan, *1955 album*.)

This proves lust can, in fact, turn into love! We were no longer 'Mr & Mrs Just Met', we now shared delicate kisses.

My American Boy

Fancy That!

Chapter 4

Back to my flight

Maybe, as I waited to board my flight, my annoyance directed towards 'Mr & Mrs Just Met' was predominately my own jealously kicking in. How I would love to feel like that again. In fact, what would you give to be in the position of 'Mr & Mrs Just Met'? It's such a wonderful experience to be in a new consensual relationship, to explore and touch a new body, a new soul. I was honoured to experience this with A4; I am so lucky I did. The excitement of having that rapport between you can be electrifying – but only if you experience the 'Perfect Stimulation' ladies.

Perfect stimulation

Wham bam, thank you ma'am, is not really in the female vocabulary, especially when it comes down to sex. Women love a build up to intercourse.

Guys need the direct approach. Just touch his cock, and the sooner the better (the more points under your belt, ladies). Get his pants undone, squeeze it, and blow job the deed in hand. The more saliva the better, girlies.

A woman's needs are quite different to those of a man. Ladies need build up, gentle stimulation, a 'slow hand'. With slow stimulation, his finger and/or tongue will help increase and heighten your pleasure.

Our nipples obviously become erect, our vaginas become excited and can get extremely warm and wet. Our vaginas become so moist, we could grow our own forest moss, wild mushrooms or even a Himalayan honeysuckle in there. Himalayan honeysuckle thrives on moisture by the way!

The more sexual teasing the better. This is key for a woman as it puts us into a marvellous, seductive, hypnotic state of mind; it blows us away.

The most important thing to a woman is getting into an enjoyable position. Then, it better be bloody slow to start off with; women want a nice, steady rhythm so she can reach orgasm. Some men like to move their women into other positions before even allowing us to reach our peak. It's like us women, in the middle of that blow job, bam, I think I'll move him into another position and start again. Wrong choice! Never move your man when he is trying to climax and never move a woman.

Some guys think to 'make love' at the speed of lightning is what they need to do but no, no, no... Guys, unless your woman tells you to fuck her fast and hard, you better slow down. Am I right ladies? Of course, I am. Women need foreplay and lots of it before hand, otherwise it's just boring banging.

Guys, firstly you need to bring your cock, snake, python or whatever else you desire to call it, into the vagina, then slide it out. Get into a rhythm and tease us. Then, go for the porn 100-mile thrusting, but only if your partner is comfortable with it.

There is a lot said about the one-eyed snake hanging out of the side of his pants or his boxers in the morning. He is waiting for some action and raring to go. He is enthusiastic to empty his oil, but the Himalayan honeysuckle needs watering first. None of us want a dry fuck in the morning.

Guys, use your snake to slither and slide, just like your finger should be used when fingering the vagina. If it's dry, use saliva or lubricant. A man needs to decelerate (go slower), and a woman needs to accelerate her man's gearbox, but not all at once. Take turns and enjoy. Women's sexual pleasure juices are brought on through arousal, but a man's semen needs to empty out ASAP. ('Slow Hand', the Pointer Sisters, *Black and White*, 1981.)

Did you know?

Men love surprises just as much as women do. You don't have to stick to the same thing, by lying on your back, with legs wide open. Get into a new position, have sex in the car and do it at lunch time rather than bedtime. Ask him to fuck you in the bathroom (but remember to apply lubricant up there before you enter the bathtub or shower ladies) or touch his cock under the table while out at dinner; that should stimulate his appetite and, get him excited. Have sex in the greenhouse! you could water the plants first, then bend over as if to sow some seeds into pots.

Once your man knows his woman is satisfied, he will become that tiger and feel powerful and competent with you.

He will, of course, become your puma, your snow leopard...excited and strong, and he will be purring, ladies!

Back at the airport

Glancing again at the caressing couple, 'Mr & Mrs Just Met', I smiled to myself with a mischievous grin. Hmm, that won't bloody last. How could it, when sitting to my right was 'Mr & Mrs Grumpy'? Probably only married for six months and already arguing over purchases of duty-free. Let's now introduce them to you, as I mentioned previously, I named them 'Mr & Mrs Duty-Free'.

Opposite me sat an older couple, probably in their sixties. He was dressed in a pair of old corded 1970 trousers, which looked like they were meant to be black but had faded in the wash and now resembled a stonewashed grey. He was also wearing a black sweater, but what amused me the most was his tartan Paddington bear scarf. His wife had irregular teeth and resembled Roald Dahl's Mrs Twit. From the left-over food surrounding their mouths, they looked like they had just eaten wormy spaghetti. Not a word was spoken between them. They looked utterly miserable. Where had all that passion gone? Probably south, there was certainly no visible magnetism between them anymore. I suspect, from past experiences, no one is ever 100% happy.

So, should you stay with one partner or seek numerous affairs? Are you seeking an affair to feel loved or to feel infatuation once again? Maybe, the real question, churning around in your head, is this: is what I am doing, seeking, or desiring – having an affair – wrong? Am I hurting my partner to satisfy my own needs?

The answer is yes. It's insanely wrong if you have morals and, of course, your partner will feel betrayed. It's not something you can sweep under the carpet once found out. Infidelity ruins many relationships, without doubt. It breaks up families and destroys children.

Maybe, you're having a heart to heart with yourself? He/she will never find out, I've got this. Really? There seems to be something in the phrase 'to thine own self be true' (*Hamlet*, William Shakespeare). What you desire, you can also fear. You can choose to experience it, if you so wish; however, your decision will give you an opportunity to grow and learn. Do you know your true self, what you really desire?

Everyone has thoughts of having sex with another (meaning someone other than their partner) at some point. It could have been someone you met on a plane, train, bus, up a mountain skiing, standing in the supermarket queue, or waiting at the dentist. It may have been that tour guide who escorted you through the desert, the person who took you to hospital, booked your flight, or looked into your eyes as they sang their heart out at your favourite concert, or it could be an old romance you had at seventeen years old.

Did you know?

Firefly femme fatales lure unsuspecting males of other species to their death. One group of female fireflies called Photuris have the nickname *femme fatales* and they sneak on to a spider's web to steal their prey.

'She captured him on a spider's web, she eats him alive for his poison she does not produce'.

Maybe some of us women are like the female firefly, flashing our light twice to confirm we are ready for sex, but then hundreds fly towards us, but we can only have one of them. Just like sperm, only one succeeds. You can have just one true partner unless you are into having affairs. Many feel it is a masculine trait to have numerous affairs but, hey, us ladies are also capable of the dirty deed.

Whether or not you choose this path is purely your own decision. There is no room for maybe. However, you must accept the consequences of your actions. So, should you have an affair? Only you can answer because it will be you who must live with it.

An affair can give you a temporary break. Break your marriage, break someone else's or put you on a new path. You can become the new you that you wanted to be, have your eyes opened or purely be taught not to mess with fire. Whichever applies, you will learn your lesson: hard, harsh or in the moment.

So, you have that affair, you leave, and your current relationship ends. You cry, you close the door on your past, but you didn't mean to. You hurt your partner, or they hurt you. Hmm, really. Just when you think you've got away with hurting someone. Bang. Karma hits you when you least expect.

Many will have already experienced an affair, and the consequences that followed, but many others have no need for an affair, because they have found their soul mate. But when we speak of a 'soul mate', is this purely someone with whom we share a sexual relationship, calling them our romantic partner? Is it possible for a soul mate to be just that? Or does there have to be a connection between two people that goes beyond physical attraction? You feel you've known them all your life, there's an invisible energy that connects you. You both like the same things, you both laugh at the same jokes, you feel that lovely feeling when you're around them and you have the same goals in life.

Or maybe you feel the need to connect with them and you're fooling yourself? That beautiful soul you were totally into has turned sour. The relationship is not really what you make out to your friends; your partner intimidates you, threatens you, puts you down and makes you feel like you need to escape, or they simply do something so bad you must walk away.

Many don't have the funding to seek a relationship counsellor. This is where the system lets us down but, hey, not all is lost. I know when I needed professional help, in my first marriage, I could not afford it, but was lucky enough to fund a few sessions via a family member. I got divorced (divorce number 1), retrieved my dignity and carried on.

Becoming a counsellor takes years to achieve and I have a lot of respect for them. However, the moment you sit in front of a trained counsellor, they all ask similar questions, like; how does that make you feel? To be honest, a counsellor's job is to guide people through their own thoughts so they can see and make their own decisions.

Sometimes, simply writing down your wants and needs helps you to find the answers you are seeking. It lessens the need for expensive counsellors and puts you back in the driving seat.

However, things can get out of hand and, if they do, having a qualified counsellor to support you is a necessity.

Sometimes, only you can work it out and other times you need the assistance of a qualified professional. Or you just need a good friend or family member to offer sound advice. You basically need to feel empowered.

Life is like a film. You are the actor and have been given your lines. The film is made up of many experiences on your journey. The experiences, whether good or bad, are yours to keep and for you to pass on the knowledge you have gained to others. It is your learning curve.

It's like getting on the same train every day, and getting off at the same station but, sometimes, we fall asleep and miss our stop. We find ourselves experiencing another train station. Some people no longer need to ride the train because they think they have achieved everything they wanted to do in life but, is it not true, even when you achieve your goals, you always want more? No one is ever 100% content, always searching, at some point in their life, for more. So, what's next in your life? What do you want? ('What's Happening Next?', Gina Foster, *Luxury Soul,* 2019.)

Couples that stay together

Okay, so before I get slated, yes, many couples are happy and remain together for life. I hear a song coming my way! ('Spend My Life With You', Eric Benét, *A Day in the Life,*1999.)

Seriously, they are the lucky ones because I believe their relationship must have a lot of laughter. Couples that stay together have a strong bond and seem to tease each other in a light-hearted way, even when they argue. When there is conflict, they are still pleasant to one another, which reminds them they still like each other. When you stop laughing together, you are more likely to break up;[that is my belief, or it may just boil down to sheer luck.

It seems that early in a marriage, anger and contempt is highly toxic and can lead to divorce and separation, but later in marriage, once laughter no longer lives in the relationship, it is a clear route to divorce, separation or years of unhappiness.

Most people will say its lack of communication that separates couples, but the biggest aspect of divorce, I believe, is lack of laughter. Yes, communication is key, but laughter outweighs all. So, if you are looking for a potential partner, you'd better explore their funny bone. Does this mean if they don't have one, you are doomed? Of course, you bloody are.

I am no psychotherapist but, please, trust the spiritual intuition that lives inside you. Do you really want to live with a boring, miserable old fart? We have all ignored it and regretted it at some point in our lives. You may have met someone and thought, there are five things I don't like about this person but there are twenty things I love about them. Hmm, intuition alarm bell going off - can you hear it? Maybe you have ignored it because the twenty things you love outweigh the five things you hate. Big mistake!

Another person may like the five things you don't, but if you don't like them, you will never change them, and if you think you will, then you are mistaken. You may be in a relationship with a narcissist or maybe you are the narcissist. A narcissistic person is controlling. Many people are in a narcissistic relationship, some slightly, while others are being totally controlled.

Some people have never heard of the narcissistic personality, but it does exist and needs to be addressed if you are a victim. Hidden underneath the surface of a very sociable and smooth operator is the superego narcissist. They drain your energy, period.

As I stated, I believe the key to happiness is laughter, it releases stress and has even been known to help beat cancer and other diseases. Therefore, if you have no laughter and are being controlled by narcissistic behaviour, maybe it's time to move on.

But remember this: if your intuition, your gut instinct, is telling you something, it is probably right. It boils down to our spirit, our higher self that we need to listen to and recognise what we are being told. We either choose to listen or ignore it. ('Free To Be Me', Feat. Norman Brown, Lindsey Webster, *Luxury Soul*, 2019.)

I have been told, for a great read on narcissistic behaviour you can't get any better than:

Should I Stay or Should I Go? and *Don't You Know Who I Am?*

(Both books by Ramani Durvasula)

Chapter 5

Fun in the sky

My attention was brought back to my imminent departure by an announcement over the tannoy. Our flight had been called and boarding had commenced. The stampede began. Typically, all passengers strived to get to the front of the queue.

I peeled my fat bottom away from the fake leather seat, tickets, and passport in hand, and peered through the large airport windows at the picturesque scene. The exclusive night-time runway was illuminated with bright, orange, and green lights that reflected off beads of water on the window from the recent downpour of rain.

As I stepped outside onto the tarmac, I looked up at the night sky and closed my eyes for a second. I needed a minute to collect myself before securing my position in line to board the plane.

Once inside, there was a surplus of bodies still trying to find their seats. It resembled a battleground, with everyone pushing and shoving. There was the usual rush to see who could place their hand luggage in the plastic overhead compartments first. Our childish ways never cease to amaze me.

Managing to secure my seat, I continued to observe my fellow passengers. The couple from the departure lounge were still bickering over their duty-free purchases as they eventually took their seats but, much to my amazement, 'Mr & Mrs Just Met' were seated just behind them still whispering sweet nothings.

The overture between the two couples was like a mix of heavy rock and an instrumental of chilled love songs. I just wanted to throw a bucket of ice-cold water over them all. After all, we were destined for the North Pole. God, these people were enough to send you crazy.

I turned my attention away from them briefly and thought about my trip. I was to chair a conference on spirituality experiences at The Grand Ice Hotel in Luztoff.

To be honest, I was feeling a little anxious. I was, however, excited at the prospect of seeing the aurora borealis, predominantly seen in high-latitude regions. The northern lights had always intrigued me. I was hopeful to see these mystical lights dance upon the sky in nature's most spectacular eerie light show and I so wanted to be captivated by this phenomenon. For now, I just had to get through the flight.

Toilet brigade

The seat belt sign came on, accompanied by the take-off announcement. Ms Swagalicious, aka 'air stewardess' (step to the left, step to the right, darlings), strutted her stuff as she imparted a wealth of inflight information. She was 5ft 7, slim with thick, auburn hair, neatly secured in a bun. She had a full face of pretty freckles with a golden tan, and beautiful white teeth. Her skin carried the faint aroma of lemon infused with jasmine that wafted through the cabin.

I must have nodded off to sleep and, before I realised, we were in flight. However, the seat belt sign was still activated. Ping! The sign illuminated green, oh God. Here we go...the herd were off. There was now a race to get to the toilet, the silver metal throne.

What is it about aeroplane toilets? As soon as the seat belt sign is turned off, it seems everyone wants to have 'a chat with the captain', an Australian term for visiting the toilet. When I was a child, I was told by my mother that when we flush a toilet in the sky (a plane toilet, obviously) our faeces are sucked out of the plane and the air altitude evaporates it. That's a myth. Can you imagine flying excrement falling from the sky at you?

Flying shit!

'Hey mum, I'm just popping up the road to get milk.'

'Okay, love, be careful. The weather forecast predicts shit missiles today with an overcast of diarrhoea. Don't forget your yellow moisture protection Macintosh, your shit shield armour (cod piece jock strap) and your reinforced, lubricant umbrella.'

Can you imagine plane excrement just flying around and hitting you? Imagine if our weathermen and women forecast an easterly wind of curry poo followed by frankfurter droppings.

'Wednesday predicts an improvement of light westerly winds of shit but on Thursday the temperature will be heating up to 25^c of Singapore poo noodles. The weekend looks bright, low clouds with short bursts of urination.'

Can you imagine a sweltering day with fans running to cool you down?

'Hey, Jack, fancy a game of golf today before the shit hits the fan?'

Come on, we all know plane faeces are siphoned into sealed tanks and sucked out by the ground staff when the plane lands. Of course, the ground staff don't literally suck out the shit; they use a large vacuum.

Arctic Narwhal!

Continuing to observe the toilet brigade as they rushed to get to the throne, I remained securely anchored in my seat. I sat with my thoughts and considered my expectations of life.

Being once a slim, UK size 10, everything fitted nicely and there I was sitting on a plane in economy seating and now ballooned from the air pressure. I was horrified; how had this happened? Peering down at myself, I concluded that I now resembled an Arctic narwhal with a pointed nose or, to be a little more realistic, I was more like a 100-ton walrus. Fat rolls were an understatement as my blubber kept me warm. It seems plane seats are too small and not designed for fully grown adults or women with curves.

The air stewardess was swaggering her swagger, as she walked down the aisle distributing drinks.

Seated next to me, to my right, was a slim, previous version of myself. Dressed in black, making her appear even thinner, was this stunning woman with long, golden hair. She had almond-shaped, green eyes emphasised by delicately placed, black eyeliner which made her appear mysteriously sexy. She had boobs to die for and a waistline which enhanced her structured abs. She resembled a nymph, a mythological beautiful maiden. She looked like she had originated from the Nymphaeum (originally a public fountain) in Petra, Jordan, now shaded by a wild pistachio tree. Here, the Bedouin people still reside in caves, with their black eyeliner, looking sexier than sexy. They enjoy a simple way of life that harks back to biblical times.

The nymph woman had ordered a drink which was served with a packet of peanuts on a neat, little, white placemat bearing the inscription 'North Pole'.

'Excuse me,' I said, as I caught the attention of Ms Swagalicious. 'Could I have a red wine, please.'

All the while, 'Nymphy' remained by my side, slim and stunning, and there I was, voluptuous but still sexually attractive.

Before I knew it, my plastic wine glass and freezing cold wine had arrived. It was time to adjust my expanding seat belt which was too bloody tight for my expanded waistline. I put it down to the doughnut and fizzy drink I had eaten earlier that morning; totally bloated me out!

Well, that went down a treat; my once full glass was now empty. I reached out and placed my plastic glass into the back of the seat located in front of me. You know that place where the sick bag used to live and where we all stuff dirty tissues, sweet wrappers and whatever else we can cram in there. Maybe a used condom, chewing gum or a dirty diaper/nappy? Whatever happened to the 'sick bag', that brown paper bag everyone had access to on flights (well, at least in the 1980s). They were still very much mandatory. Have people ceased to suffer travel sickness or are they just stuffed full of ginger to alleviate the need for a sick bag.

Have you ever considered the mysterious departure of sick bags, huh? Well, they do still exist but are under lock and key. They are kept with the air stewards and no longer deposited in the rear seat pocket in front of you to cut down on cost. So many people fly these days, they have adjusted to flying and airlines do not allow drunk passengers on board, but hey. Guess what? Some airlines still use them and deposit them with their news magazines.

Fancy that!

The Pussy Wink

As I reclined backwards in my seat, the most gorgeous 'Mr Good-Looking' caught my eye as he swept down the aisle. It was like he was walking on air. Where did he appear from? My heart started to race, and my eyes couldn't stop fixating on this guy's handsome, chiselled jawline and defined cheek bones. He had the most amazing piercing blue eyes and chestnut brown hair, not to mention his 'come to bed' stubble, just enough to tickle your fancy if you know what I mean.

Fun in the sky

A little bit of what you fancy does you good, ladies and gents. Is this the reason men grow beards? It adds to our vaginal stimulation, we should call them 'cum beards'. Maybe Santa got it right, he's had a 'cum beard' for years. I'm sure he tickles Mrs Claus, making her cum. She probably bakes him Christmas pudding every year, served with cum sauce. To be honest, I'm not so keen on 'cum beards', stubble yes, but not beards.

It seems there were thousands of Sir Walter Raleigh's walking the planet in 2019 with their 'cum beards' and vapes (I wonder what Sir Walter Raleigh would think if he was able to come back and see his discovery of tobacco being changed into a cherry flavour vape).

Everywhere I looked there were more and more of them appearing. It was like we had been invaded by 'cum beards' and there I was thinking 2019 was the Chinese Year of the Dog.

Without anyone noticing and being turned on by 'Mr Good-Looking', I commenced my pelvic floor exercise (or as I like to call it, the 'pussy wink'). It's like having a secret mini orgasm that no one knows you are experiencing.

The pelvic floor muscles can hold on to a guy's cock and pulsate it. It's like sucking through a straw and letting go. Women can all do it, just as guys think about sex every minute, we can do the 'pussy wink' wherever and whenever.

So, what is the 'pussy wink', you might ask? Kegel exercises, otherwise known as pelvic floor exercises, help to strengthen the muscles around your bladder, vagina, back passage and… drum roll, ladies…his penis. It can help stop incontinence, treat prolapse and even lead to better sex by achieving great orgasms.

The best way to feel your pelvic floor muscles is to stop the flow of urine when you go to the toilet. Basically, you are pulling those muscles up then letting go. It's about clenching then releasing. If your guy can waggle his cock, making his penis move up and down when it's erect, then he is using his pelvic floor muscles.

When you wink at someone, it can indicate assurance, playfulness, a liking towards them or even instigate sex. To wink, you need to close the eyelid (clench) then open the eyelid (release). So, if you imagine your eyelid 'upside down', placed in your vagina, ladies, and it closes, then opens, you are doing the 'pussy wink'.

Get your pussies winking to avoid being forced to wear those pee leak pads.

Dough!

My attention was drawn back to 'Mr Good-Looking' and how he aroused my senses.

I fancied some mints and reached out for my handbag on the floor in front of me. Not only could I not reach my bag, but I also had to take off the blasted seat belt that I had managed to adjust to a voluptuous, expanding, supersize waistline.

Struggling and fiddling, I finally managed to retrieve it. With bag in hand, I reached inside to locate a packet of mints but, to my amazement, I also found a block of playdough. How the hell did that get in there? It must be one of the last batches I made for my grandchildren. We often made it with flour, water, cream of tartar, vegetable oil and salt. I was meant to drop it in to them before I left for the airport; damn!

I love the feel of homemade playdough, it's one of those satisfying moments like popping bubble wrap or getting into bed with fresh clean sheets. The dough felt flexible and somewhat durable, so I separated a piece from the block and started to fondle it.

Oblivious of fellow passengers, my vivid imagination took over. I might have gone overboard in my excitement. It felt like the forbidden fruit was to emerge and burst their juices. Well, my juice was building in my panties, baby, probably from too much 'pussy winking'. My fondled dough was heating up in my sweaty palms.

My attention was quickly drawn back to reality. Nymphy-slim-bitch got up from her seat and ventured to the back of the plane. Leaning forward and peering to my right, looking back, I watched her walk down the aisle as her perfect derriere headed in the direction of the toilet. Phew! Thank God for that; she was gone.

Still holding my dough between my fingers, I accidently dropped the dough on Nymphy's now empty seat. The slim bitch never returned. Had she headed off in search of Petra, to return home to the Nymphaeum. Was this true? Nymphs love water, don't they? Or maybe she was just hiding in the silver metal throne room, waiting for action.

Mr Latino

In my vision I started to see a strange formation of lights like the aurora borealis (northern lights). A swirling mass of electrifying colours appeared from the dough that accidently lay upon Nymphy's seat.

The dough was morphing into what resembled a man, a Latino man. 'Mr Latino' was tanned, with dark black hair, slicked back with grease. His eyes were hypnotic, as if they were inviting me to come to his bed. He wore tight, stretchy, black trousers that enhanced his tight, peachy bum, with an open, unbuttoned red satin shirt. You know... typical sexy tango attire.

As he drew closer, he made me feel alive again. He embraced me, taking my hand to interlock my fingers with his. He was beckoning me to engage with him, and engage I did as he danced me up the plane's aisle.

He gently spun me around, like I was spinning his web. He turned and gave me the sexiest wink ever (it was no 'pussy wink' though). As we shared a moment of intimacy, he flicked his foot between my legs. Glancing into my eyes, pulling me closer, he placed a piece of lime crunch chocolate into my mouth. His synchronised movements and breathing had a similar rhythm to that of tantric sex.

But oh, no, 'Mr Latino' was fading. My morphed hunk was disappearing before my eyes. He had started to sweat, and then harden from the air pressure, but not in the way I would like him to have done. He hardened so much, he cracked into pieces and vanished. ('Perhaps, Perhaps, Perhaps', Halie Loren, *They Oughta Write a Song*, 2008.)

Chapter 6

Tango or Tantric sex

The tango originated in the 1880s along the River Plate (Rio de la Plata), the natural border between Argentina and Uruguay, and was frequently practised in brothels and bars. The tango is a vibrant and playful dance. It is played out between two people and has a rich form of expression and connection. The Argentine tango is deeply passionate and requires the participants to desire, understand, and converse with the person they are dancing with.

In tango there is a leader and follower. Through the embrace, the leader offers an invitation to the follower. Both try to maintain harmony and connection through their embrace. Just like tantric sex, the tango is a collaborative process that encourages a respectful development of sensitivity, clarity and trust. Tango, like tantric sex, is about sharing a moment of intimacy and understanding.

Tantric sex is a form of slow sex that increases intimacy and creates a mind/body connection which can lead to powerful orgasms. It's a physical pleasure but extremely spiritual.

Tantra is about being conscious of your connection to your soul, your body and your connection to love. It is a Hindu practice over 5,000 years old. Tantra is about weaving and expanding energy, just like the dance of the tango; weaving in and out as you discover the intimate sexiness of the dance.

Why would you opt for a quick romp when you could enjoy a session of tantric sex? Tantra is a deep connection of

Tango or Tantric sex

loving sex and moving energy throughout your body. It's all about slowing the breath down. Sit face to face on the floor (naked, of course). Look into each other's eyes and let go of your inhibitions. There is no room for shyness here. Inhale as your partner exhales.

Massage is particularly good, and lots of it, but remember, the aim is to intensify your partner's senses. Build them to a peak and then pull back a little, don't go all the way until you are both ready. The longer you pull back, the longer this prolongs sex. In this way, you can keep the pleasure going for hours.

Remember, the breath is so important. Most women breathe too quickly as they are climaxing. Orgasm will last longer and be more intense if you learn to control your breath simultaneously. Otherwise, you can always dance the tango naked or simply opt for lots of 'pussy wink'. Just like the tango, tantra is about teasing.

Farting and Flatulence

I tried to capture the attention of the air stewardess again as I wriggled uncomfortably in my seat. Feeling somewhat deprived, I said, 'Excuse me, may I have another red wine, please.'

At last, she noticed my request. Swagalicious handed me another clear plastic glass with a small bottle of full-bodied red wine followed by a little packet of peanuts. Oh no! Not more bloody peanuts. *Nope, I am not going to do it,* I thought, as I automatically ripped the packet of nuts open and stuffed them into my mouth.

Now with salty lips and an added thirst for wine, my digestion suddenly went into overload. Oh, my goodness, the turbulence had begun and just as the seat belt sign was activated.

Being fastened to my seat like that, as if I were wearing a 1900s' corset, I could see my tummy ballooning. My stomach was feeling extremely windy as I ballooned even more. It was like a hurricane was about to burst out from me.

It had to be those bloody peanuts. No, oh no, it had started. I now needed to release gas. And lots of it. My stomach gases needed some form of escape. All I could think about was getting to the toilet, but that was currently out of bounds due to the blasted seat belt sign. There was turbulence in the sky and certainly mega turbulence going on in my tummy.

Too late! I just had to expel my gas. You ask, was that ladylike? Not bloody likely. Having no choice in the matter, it was either squeeze my legs together or block my arse hole completely.

Quickly reaching for some dough, I pulled and stretched another piece and discreetly positioned it under my arse. It was such a relief as I reclined once again into my seat. Thank God for that. It had soaked up the noise and the ghastly scent as it plugged my backside.

No smell, no noise, just pure relief. I suppose it was a bit like those flatulence filtering garments you can insert into your panties, ladies.

Feeling more relaxed and peering out of the plane window, another thought entered my mind. *What if the dough I had just plugged my arse with cracks open mid-flight, just like 'Mr Latino' did?* The smell would escape and expel to my fellow passengers. Maybe they would like it. Hmm. I could market this; bottled fart, with undertones of peanuts and base notes of red grape. So, when you really don't like someone, you can send them a 'message in a bottle'.

A bottle of farts. Take that arsehole. Wink!

Did you know (Vaginal farts)

A vaginal fart is called a 'Queef'.

What's that all about, ladies, when you fart from your vagina? No, really. Have you ever discussed this with your girlfriend, partner, or doctor? I have often experienced a vaginal fart. It's like a bubble, a poof of air that puffs its way through your vagina and it is very often associated with having sex and making sounds like you are farting. Your pussy fart can catch you unawares, especially when first with a new partner, which can be extremely embarrassing. This is air rushing out of your vagina, while a fart is gas coming out of your butt.

Farts are smelly, as they are a result of bacteria breaking down and being released as gases from your digestive system. Queefs do not come from digestion; they are basically caused by air travelling up the vagina and then sneaking out when you least expect it. They do not smell but they do make noises like a butt fart. Queefs can be embarrassing but are normal.

Fancy that, hey!

Mr Funny

After a short period of relaxation, the stomach cramps, bloating and inflammation of my stomach lining subsided. I gracefully pulled the plug of dough from my backside and commenced fondling the stinky chunk. Yes, disgusting you might say. Smoke suddenly appeared, swirling into the empty seat next to me (Nymphy's, of course).

But this was not normal smoke; it seemed to get denser, icy cold with strange sounds of firecrackers. It made me giggle. Morphing from the smoke appeared 'Mr Funny'.

His character and appearance were clown-like. His tummy was extremely large, and he had a distinguished, big red nose, the surface of which resembled potholes (well, craters really). His face was covered in age spots. He had gaps in his teeth, and I think he had tried to glue them together, but the tooth-*paste* he used had failed. Maybe he should visit the dentist more often; they are great problem solvers and so good at getting to the root of the problem.

His name was Norman, and he was one of the funniest guys I had ever met. Norman told me how he would visit brothels - huh! Smiling, with the most mischievous grin, I asked him why. Norman told me that, at the brothel, he would stick his cock into a drilled hole in a cemented wall.

'Why would you do that, Norman?' I asked.

'Because, if I stick my erection through a hole in the wall, and I don't mean the ATM, it can be used as a dick hole for a blow job and you don't have to see the person and they, in turn, don't have to see my ugly face. They only see my dipstick…dick.'

He also told me he thought men should have 'cocknballograms'.

'Cocknballograms! What the hell are they, Norman?'

Women have mammograms right! Well, then imagine men sticking their cocks between two plates of metal, what!

Don't worry, Mr Franklin, we'll only be squashing your cock for a few minutes, it won't be too uncomfortable!

I laughed so much. I must have badly needed it. Laughter is always infectious and is extremely contagious. The saying is true, 'laugh and the whole world laughs with you'. Laughter decreases stress hormones and triggers the release of endorphins, the body's natural feel-good chemicals, thus promoting healing.

Of course, some people laugh when something is not meant to be funny. This is called 'nervous laughter' and is often known as fake laughter that heightens the awkwardness of a situation. People sometimes laugh when they witness an accident or other people's pain (inappropriate laughter) especially when someone falls over and looks like a complete idiot.

I think it is one of the funniest forms of laughter because you know (deep down) you shouldn't be laughing but as you try to hold back, it becomes completely uncontrollable. When it gets seriously past that stage, then come the tears, coughing and an outburst of belly laughter. We have all done it at some time in our lives.

Did you know?

An interesting and, surprisingly, factual condition is having a 'giggle fit' otherwise known as a 'gelastic seizure' or 'gelastic epilepsy'.

This is a rare type of seizure that involves a sudden burst of energy, like laughing, which is uncontrollable. In fact, my daughter 'London' suffers from this condition. She freezes with laughter and goes into a laughing seizure. Fancy that, hey!

Going back to Norman, aka 'Mr Funny'. After exposing his moon face at me, and now quickly pulling up his pants, his existence seemed to be short-lived.

A boy around six years old looking like one of the Munsters - Eddie Munster to be precise - wearing a red Santa's hat, ran up the aisle and stuck a large plastic fork into the bottom of 'Mr Funny'. Norman seemed to go into a 'giggle fit', froze, and vanished in a cloud of dense, grey smoke. 'Mr Funny' had departed.

Let's get sexy

The cabin lights were dipped, it was very dark outside, and blankets and pillows had been distributed by Swaga. Now what?

Thinking it might calm me down, I decided to listen to some music and reached for my earphones that, of course, had been placed into the same place where the sick bag lives.

Peering down at my armrests, I identified the radio channel controls available to me.

I was in the mood for smooth jazz (something a bit funky, too). Hmm, Incognito would go down a treat. In my mind, I heard the vibrant and tantalising sound of 'Spellbound and Speechless'. ('Spellbound and Speechless', Incognito, *100º and Rising*, 1995.)

Without a doubt, Incognito are pure magic, pure talent, and pure funk. They can certainly fill you with a frisson of excitement; so you become enraptured and intoxicated by the bewitching thrill of music.

My ears pricked up, and I was transported to another level as I started to embrace the smooth sound of sex. Who could do this better than the legend himself, Mr Barry White, with his 'Love Making'. Frisson had certainly started as I reclined back into my seat. My eyelids felt heavy, and so, I closed them. A sigh of sex surrounded me. The tone of 'Love Making' pulsated through my entire body. If only my fellow passengers could feel my frisson, not to mention my 'pussy wink'. I was on fire; everyone knows frisson is like a skin orgasm, right? Barry's electrifying voice had transported me to sexual heaven.

His hypnotic voice was certainly deeply sexy.

I was also experiencing 'numinous'; a kind of spirituality. It felt so good I couldn't help feeling there was a spiritual element to the music. Could I have been having a numinous-frisson experience?

Chapter 7

So let's explore frisson

Frisson (pronounced *free-sawn*) is a French term meaning 'aesthetic chills'. If you are like me, you had probably never heard of this word, let alone know its meaning. However, I was aware that I often experienced a beautiful feeling pouring over my skin, even as a child, but I never questioned it, I just enjoyed it. But what exactly is this feeling I have been so lucky to experience, not once, but many times during my life?

This feeling of frisson is one of immense tuning into oneself and often happens when you listen to music, watch a film, admire art and, occasionally, when someone stands close to you. It's when you find the one piece of music that moves you and resonates with your soul. It's a beautiful feeling you just can't explain. It's almost spiritual. It's a wave of pleasure running through your body, as if inner energy has awakened. You feel chills running up your spine and goosebumps dancing on your skin. You are stimulated with frisson and those few seconds or minutes are simply out of this world. It's like you are having a 'skin orgasm', a magnetic wave running all over your body that you just don't want to stop.

Scientists are still researching the phenomenon of frisson. I am no scientist, but I can personally say I love the frisson feeling and wanted to share it with you. You may have experienced it yourself or wondered what the hell it was.

Frisson, I believe, is something you interact with, that your soul feels and

So let's explore frisson

resonates with on an energy level. It raises our electrical vibrations within our spiritual soul. It awakens and tunes into what our spirit, our soul, likes. It's like tasting your favourite food and your body immediately knows your taste buds are delighted, and you feel good.

Or, perhaps, you might experience frisson when listening to a piece of music you like. Maybe the music is on the same frequency your body is attuned to and it opens up and says, 'Hey, I like that piece of music, I'm going to give you a sign all over your body to give you the thumbs up'.

Just like when you are sad, your body produces tears, when you are attuned into the frequency your body likes, the music lifts your vibrations, your frequency raises the bar, interacts, and says, 'Hey, Dude, are you feeling it, that frisson feeling?'

Maybe the next time you experience it, you may want to investigate what music that was, what frequency, what musical notes made you feel that way. Or were you at an art gallery and really felt a frisson of excitement.

I sometimes get that frisson feeling when listening to the string orchestra family such as the violin or cello, but I feel it also depends on a person's general spiritual vibration.

I don't believe everyone has the same vibration that they resonate with. That is possibly why some experience frisson more frequently and others never do. Maybe we should rename frisson and call it 'funky sensation'. ('Funky Sensation', Gwen McCrae, 1981.)

Mr Lover

Reaching for more dough, not knowing what I would do with it, I located a decorated fleece blanket and placed it over my body for warmth. My blanket was grey with imprints of Arctic skies.

As I kneaded and thumbed the dough, it felt warm, putty-like, pliable but not sticky. The dough, once again, took over as I worked it into a rhythm on my thighs. The rhythm increased as the music intensified momentum, it was all a bit tantric. A large aura of red petals swirled around me; morphing had begun...revealing 'Mr Lover'.

'Mr Lover' characterised sex on legs (the crème de la crème) thus, temptation was about to take over me. He was of Caribbean descent with chocolate brown skin, deep brown 'come to bed' eyes and muscles to die for. He was a slick dresser and held a distinctive cane that distinguished his personality. The mysterious cane was encrypted with the twelve signs of the zodiac, meaning he had experienced every sign sexually and had no problem going round each sign many times, again and again. He just loved sex; whether it was with someone who was married, divorced, or single, his goal was to satisfy, and satisfy he did.

He gently removed my earphones, took my hand, and smiled. He then led me to the back of the plane, all the while serenading me with the sound of 'Let's Get It On'. After all, would you deny a bit of Marvin Gaye to heat things up?

Pulling me into the silver metal throne room, sometimes referred to as the bathroom, 'Mr Lover' engaged the 'In Use' sign as he locked the door behind us.

We were both startled by some action in the toilet pan. It was Nymphy swirling around. Was I fazed by this? Certainly not, and my black stiletto heel slammed the throne's lid upon her now sinking head. I was, however, amazed to discover the toilet was larger than the average rest room on an aeroplane.

My attention turned back to 'Mr Lover'. His once south facing rocket was now northbound and firing up for action. He was so compelling I could feel his magnificent erection pressing against my hip as he slowly turned my torso to direct my back against the door, thrusting against me as he simultaneously kissed and licked my neckline and décolletage. I felt like I had just been gifted some incredible sexual confidence. I am sure you, too, have experienced this sexually confident feeling at some stage.

Having my hands held to ransom above my head, and loving it; it was driving me wild not to touch him. I wanted more, and more he gave as he pulled up my skirt and pulled my panties sideways, sliding his strong fingers inside my moist vagina. 'Pussy wink' was blissfully engaged.

Beads of sweat appeared between my breasts as my white lace blouse was ripped open. Erect nipples were then revealed as my breasts were released from my tight bra. Trusting him completely, I wanted more as he continued to kiss me intensely while fingering my now very lubricated vagina. Blood pulsated round my trembling body as he continued to excite me in a way I had never experienced before.

In the heat of the moment, he pulled down my panties. Sweat was dripping off us both. His fired-up rocket entered my love tunnel. Fucking me respectfully, his ejaculation was like a whale's blowhole. I had just experienced his sexual 'whale spout'. The toilet floor was covered with a sticky white substance.

Totally out of breath, he begun thrusting inside me again, but this time his thrusting was slow. He teased me by pulling out and then recommencing his snake-like sequence.

My face was flushed as he yanked me up against the toilet sink, opening my legs wider. Looking directly into my eyes, he whispered, 'Am I hurting you?'

'No, no...don't stop,' I begged.

The weight of his muscular body scared me slightly. He was like an animal as he pressed his body against mine.

He smelt amazing too. His scent was amber, with a hint of body musk. So deliciously irresistible. It was like he had picked desert flowers and rubbed the scent over his body. I had never wanted anyone like this before.

So let's explore frisson

With music gently fading into the background, we were done. Mission complete! I smoothed down my skirt over shaking legs and re-fastened my blouse. My head was pounding from the increase in blood flow and my skin felt hot and flushed. I could smell him upon me. He had transferred his scent...

Adjusting my panties, pulling them up from my left ankle while stepping into the right leg, I noticed a lump of dough had somehow dropped on to the back of my stiletto. Quickly grabbing it, I plugged my vagina in the hope it would catch any remaining drips of sexual fluid.

Turning towards 'Mr Lover', I embraced him and sealed my lips upon his. The sex had been incredible and most desired, but then I had a thought. From the action I had just received, I would most definitely require the honeymoon treatment. A visit to the doctor would now be appropriate. Okay, I was not on honeymoon but had been fucked like I was.

Come on, ladies, honeymoon fucking quite often requires antibiotics to calm down the cystitis, thrush, or bacterial vaginosis. His fucking had certainly been deeply penetrating, and my vagina needed some natural yoghurt or a salt bath to cool it down. After all, the shafting had been amazing.

Ladies and gents, next time you visit a toilet on a plane and the floor is wet, remember, it's just 'Let's Get It On' or at least a spout of blowhole gone south.

Did you know (A whales blowhole)

A whale's blowhole is on top of its head. When they inhale, they flex a muscle which opens the blowhole, similar to a human penis when it ejaculates. So, the next time you consider that blow job (BJ), your partner may blow you away with their 'blowhole' and send you 20 feet up in the air with their whale spout.

'Fancy a BJ, Dick?'

'Not really, I wouldn't mind a whale spout though.'

Mr Spa

Exhausted from the delightful exertion, I gracefully left the toilet and commenced the walk back down the aisle to my seat. Forget the Cheshire cat, I was like the cat that had got the cream and, oh boy, the cream had followed me down the aisle, still somewhat dripping out from the dough in my panties.

As I tried to compose myself after the excitement of sexual pleasure, I thought how nice it would be to have a wonderful massage and not have to pay for it. It's no secret, we are all aware the build up to sex sometimes means 'massage first', followed by 'wifely duties'. Usually, as we lay there being fondled and stroked by our sexual partner, we have two options:

1. Embrace it and repay; settle the debt with sex.

2. Don't enjoy it, knowing what is coming next anyway; the obligational duties.

Kicking off my heels, my attention was drawn to my feet. I had just been fucked in my stilettos and, as sexy as they look ladies, you know how tremendously sore wearing heels can make your feet.

On the floor in front of me was a sausage-shaped roll of dough, poking out from the top of my handbag. I quickly picked up the dough and placed it under the soles of my feet. The coolness from the fresh dough felt like an Arctic terrain of ice, infused with the aroma of peppermint oil.

With eyes closed, I continued to massage and address the other foot. Sensing a presence, I slowly opened my eyelids. Forming before me were white swirls of electrifying lights penetrating through the dough, yet another man was morphing - 'Mr Spa'.

He appeared in a long, white laboratory coat, the scent of essential oils upon his skin. His aroma stimulated my mind and body; a mix of lavender and eucalyptus.

'Mr Spa' was somewhat handsome, mature but shy. His hands were soft and well-manicured, wide but strong. He had a Scandinavian accent, with pale skin, brown eyes, and longish, blond, wavy hair.

Having scanned him over to assess his age, he appeared to be in his mid-fifties (I bet he's good in bed; I mean, an older gentleman has experience and wants a confident woman to fuck with). I am not suggesting young people don't have great sex, but a bottle of aged wine is so much more inviting than a two-week-old bottle of prosecco - a bit of fizz!

'Mr Spa' picked up my blanket, making it into the shape of a small bolster pillow and placed it behind my head. It had begun.

His hands were strong and firm as he kneaded my neck and shoulders before positioning me forward, bringing my head to rest upon my knees. He continued down my spine using effleurage stokes, his hands in perfect alignment.

Ping! That bloody seat belt sign reappeared. Startled by the sudden tannoy announcement, 'Mr Spa' vanished just like 'Mr Lover' had done before him. Yet another man to depart my life.

Our descent was announced by the captain followed by a formal public statement that this was his last flight; he was retiring. I placed my finger upon my lips, like an emoji thinking face. Hmm. So could I give our pilot a retirement gift of lasting pleasure? Well, at least a lasting memory.

The Nymphy handshake: something for the men

It seemed Nymphy had beaten me to it. Before the retiring pilot departed his plane, he had one more check to make, his cockpit. However, he needed to urinate first.

So let's explore frisson

Entering the toilet, the one at the back of the plane, and dropping his pants, he pulled out his 'big guy' and started to urinate. A trickle emerged, turning into a strong stream of warm urine which gradually came to a halt. Flicking his cock to stop any drips, Nymphy appeared in the pan as he pressed 'flush'. She was still struggling to get out and becoming more desperate, frantically reaching out with her slimy, wet hands. As water from the flushed toilet swirled her around, she latched on to the captain's cock, giving him, an erection like no other.

The pilot now resembled a satyr, the male equivalent of a nymph. He had developed pixie ears and a large, erect, wooden trunk. He was a satyr with a cock to die for. Nymphy was a nymphomaniac, and satyr was a satyromaniac; both have hypersexuality disorders, with a sexual addiction or overactive sex drive. Now both naked, they danced their way around each other's loving arms; satyr's cock was now an incredible size.

Needless to say, the pilot would retire a happy man, but he needed to put his suit back on - he still had a plane to land.

So, the next time you are in a toilet on a plane, you may get the grab of your life or at least an imaginary 'Nymphy handshake'. May the force be with you, men!

Chapter 8

Our descent

Peering out of the window, I caught a glimpse of the Arctic sky. Snow was whipping up at speed, captured by the plane's propellers.

As we continued with our descent, dropping through grey clouds of snow, I could see miniature, twinkling, white lights. To describe the scene as Fairyland would indeed be an understatement. It was magnificent, magical, and exciting (does Santa really live here?).

The landing was smooth, as we glided over the soft, fresh snow on the runway. Icicles formed on the plane's windows.

It was dark, and the cabin was now very cold, after all, it was the middle of December.

Exchanging my heels for more suitable attire (snow boots), I followed my fellow passengers via the green exit sign. Trying not to slip on the metal ladder which led on to the snow-filled tarmac, I ventured towards the small airport of 'Luztofe' and arrived at baggage reclaim. The air temperature was bitterly cold, and I shivered despite my snow boots and an extra layer of clothes.

I could see three empty rotating carousels and a flashing red sign stating, 'delayed baggage'.

I stood for a minute propping myself up against the suitcase trolleys. As I waited, I witnessed a huddle of passengers stepping into ski-suits, putting on earmuffs to protect themselves from the cold, and applying lip balm. They were sipping hot soup from the complimentary flasks handed out as a welcome. However, there was no sign of the shrimp, caviar, or champagne, which is traditionally served to visitors on arrival.

I decided to put on my own ski-suit, which, by the way, was lime green. I looked like a fluorescent green, marshmallow tyre man. Slurping the hot vegetable and noodle soup, I gazed at the steam rising from the flask and circulating the cold air. Unfortunately, I had sipped too much soup. I gulped and choked on a noodle wedged in my throat. Coughing to help release it made me dribble, and I don't mean from my mouth.

It was only then, having slightly wet panties, that I realised I had forgotten to insert my urine leak pads into my knickers. Maybe I should have used a pelvic toner or practised a lot more 'pussy winks' throughout my life.

But I had no choice; it was either miss my luggage or proceed with wet underwear. The ice-cold air had also set into my wet knickers. My pubic hair (not being waxed) now resembled an Arctic woolly bear moth; a spiked up, prickly, Arctic caterpillar.

To insert a urine leak panty liner now would be like being pricked, and who honestly would want a prick in their ice-cold panties. At that moment, the conveyor belt in baggage reclaim sprung into life, and I collected my luggage. I witnessed a guy investigating his nose. He thought no one was looking, but I had seen him.

I was absolutely disgusted and could not believe what I was witnessing. He then had the audacity to roll and flick his snot. To top that, he went for the secret smell thing. He was aware his fingers smelt from his snot fondling but left it a few minutes to check. It's like when we do the 'bellybutton poke', the finger goes in and what do we do? We sniff our finger. No one talks about it; it seems to be a taboo subject. Can you imagine at work, in mid-conversation with a colleague?

'Hey, Gina, how was your bellybutton poke last night before you got into the shower?'

Or, 'Hey Frank, did you enjoy your bellybutton poke last night while you were sitting on the toilet?'

No one talks about doing the backside, arse wipe between the slits of your bum. The aroma (if you have poor hygiene) resembles cheese. Does that mean we all have a 'cheese arse'?

The same applies to smelly armpits. Have you ever witnessed someone sniffing their armpit? You look away in disgust but, no doubt, you will have done it yourself, at least once in your life. Such funny creatures, human beings.

Mr DIY

Struggling with my heavy luggage, I stopped to reach inside my jam-packed handbag for some gum but there I found one last piece of dough. It was quite substantial, the size of a small ball.

Placing the dough into my hands, there was a sense of great strength morphing out of it. I envisaged Es Vedra, the spiritual island rock of Ibiza, and morphing from Vedra was a spiritual man from times gone by, but dressed in today's attire.

He wore a yellow hard hat, like a builder, and blue denim jeans which contoured his muscular, animal-like bum. He was mysteriously sexy and seemed able to converse with me telepathically. His muscles were flexing through his tight, black T-shirt.

There he was, all 7 feet of him, with a tool belt hanging off his hips. I'm not sure what he was about to fix! He showed me an endless list of what he could do for me: shopping, cooking, building, plumbing, cleaning out my pipes (wink), mechanics, housework, gardening... Get my drift, ladies?

Making eye contact, he pulled some Arctic clothing out of his backpack. 'Mr DIY' commenced layering his body

Our descent

parts. Specific attention was given to his extremities. Fingers, toes and, of course, the 'big guy' – his cock. There was no way he would want frost bite there and for it to drop off.

He escorted me out of the airport, carrying my luggage, and we headed in the direction the sign was pointing, towards the huskies. The thickly furred dogs were waiting anxiously as they each, in turn (eight of them), looked round at me with their mystical, electric-blue eyes, howling and barking in the dark, snow-filled night.

Picking me up with his muscular arms and placing me securely into one of the dog sleighs, 'Mr DIY' covered me with reindeer skins and placed my luggage in the sleigh. The snow was deep and thick like a plush, white carpet.

Before I knew it, we were off. The speed of the huskies and their enchanting howling was exhilarating beyond belief. The terrain was mostly flat, as it moved through the unique formations of ice and snow, but I was jostled around in the sleigh as it went over bumps. Faster and faster we went and, as we picked up speed, I felt like I was being transported through Narnia. Snow was falling from the pine trees as we sped through the dense forest.

I could see the ice hotel flickering in the distance. It was immensely pretty with assorted green, blue and purple lights captured on the deep midnight horizon.

Snowmobile tours were out in search of the northern lights. I could hear bells jingling from a horse-drawn carriage, which crossed my path as it carried a bride, draped in a beautiful white fur cape and muff, to the ice chapel next to the frozen lake. (Yet another beautiful bride to tie the knot. Let's hope she doesn't turn into a sandwich maker and wet bathroom mat detective). There was a bridge to my right, with a large oil lantern that burned brightly, lighting the way ahead.

Our descent

Eventually, we reached my hotel, and the huskies were drawn to a slow halt. I looked up at the dazzling skyline and could see the aurora borealis flickering its mystical dance. 'Mr DIY' helped me out of the sleigh.

Trying not to fall, as I crunched my way through the deep snow, I was greeted at the hotel entrance by a Sami lady dressed in traditional Arctic costume. My luggage followed behind me and was left by the hotel porchway.

The entrance floor was covered by a dusting of powdery white snow, gently melting and glistening, from prior guests' arrivals. I could smell and taste spiced apple infused with cinnamon.

Shaking off the surplus snow that covered my lime thermal suit, I looked back to thank 'Mr DIY', but he had gone. All I could see was an empty wooden bench with holly berries entwined. Yet another man had left me!

As I reached reception, there was a notice displaying the following:

Room 1: Ice Bedroom Suite
Room 2: Numinous Encounter
Room 3: Santa's North Pole Rocket Ride
Room 4: Conference Room

Room 1 – The Ice bedroom suite

Another beautifully dressed Sami lady led me to my hotel room, the 'Ice Bedroom suite'. She closed the oval door behind her as she left, and it made a distinctive creaking sound. The door resembled an 18th century, dark oak, monastery door, worn from the constant battering of suitcases.

I looked around in amazement. My bedroom suite had been carved out of snow and ice and contained a beautifully decorated Christmas tree. The ice had been carved into detailed, magical formations of large mushrooms, and a large ice bed, laden with reindeer skins, awaited me.

I reached out and touched the ice walls, and mushroom formations with the palms of my hands. The feeling of the silky wet ice against my skin excited me. I continued tracing it with my fingertips and felt a surge of euphoria move through my whole body. This was interrupted by a knock at my bedroom door which startled me and broke my concentration. I drew close to my bed and gasped as someone entered my room. It was the 'big guy', and I don't mean A4, it was Santa himself.

He greeted me and smiled, scratching his 'cum beard'. He asked me if I needed anything and advised that his butler would shortly bring my luggage. He confirmed he was looking forward to the conference. This made me more anxious, and my nerves kicked in. He walked towards the door but then, strangely, vanished!

Room 2: Numinous encounter

In the room next door, I could hear music and went to find out what it was.

I witnessed a spiritual encounter, a psychic phenomenon.

I could see a warm glow emanating from two blue spiritual orbs circling the room. Their auras pulsated in an array of dazzling colours. The room housed a display of vibrant, beautiful, large, natural amethyst and rose quartz crystals. I could hear the distinctive sound of a Native American drum; a reflective shamanic chanting was taking place. There was a cool breeze circulating.

As the auras traced around each other, I sensed she was once his Egyptian queen and he her Native American chief – but both from different dimensions, connected by previous lifetimes. He had come back for her from another spiritual plane. They had once lived a life together that their memories had previously erased. There was to be no intercourse, just exquisite pleasure, a meeting of minds, a touching of souls, and eternal never-ending love.

Their previous existence together, their reincarnations were unbeknown to them, but he had come back for her, and she had come back for him. They were two magnificent angels. ('Buddha Bar-Orkidea Beautiful (Are You an Angel)', Morfou, 2012.)

Did you know (people you know and past life's)

People come into your life for a reason. Have you ever met someone and known you have a connection? That's because you have. Were you in contact with someone years ago and suddenly find them back in your life? That's because you have unfinished business together. Maybe an hour, a day, or the rest of your life or, perhaps, you feel that déjà vu feeling, like you knew this person you have just met, but just can't put your finger on where or when it was. Maybe you were connected in a past life together?

I would recommend looking up American author Dolores Cannon. I find her work remarkably interesting. Dolores Cannon was a hypnotherapist who specialised in past life regression, and she first discovered, what she called, 'reincarnation' in 1968. She developed her own unique method of hypnosis and called it 'Quantum Healing Hypnosis Technique' (QHHT). Her patients have described many scenes from their past lives, such as those captured in her first book, *Five Lives Remembered*, 2009. She has written many other books, such as: *The Search for Hidden Knowledge*, *The Convoluted Universe* and *Between Death and Life*. ('Déjà Vu (I've Been Here Before)', Tina Marie, *Wild and Peaceful*, 1979.)

Did you know?

The subconscious mind lies just underneath the conscious mind. QHHT allows a direct communication with our subconscious mind to answer questions and help with healing. I have never had this done but maybe, one day, I will venture back into a past life experience. Perhaps I will walk back into the spotlight and brighten up my life and find my love. Maybe A4 and I will be together in another lifetime! Perhaps I will be his spotlight once more! ('Spotlight', Tony Momrelle, *Fly*, 2013.)

Room 3: Santa's North Pole rocket ride

'Enter at you own free will', announced the notice above Room 3. Outside the door, there was a red ticket machine with the inscription 'North Pole Rocket Ride, for adults only'.

I peeped through the keyhole to reveal a startling scene. There he sat, Santa himself. He was perched upon a Christmas-themed throne decorated in gold, with green holly, red berries and white mistletoe buds. He was holding a large red and white candy cane.

Fancy That!

The room was lit with hundreds of magical white fairy lights. Red fur rugs were scattered over the dark brown, polished, wooden floorboards and a roaring fire crackled in the background. Two soldiers, dressed in red and gold, stood to attention as they watched over Santa. They were Santa's drag queens.

There were adults, hundreds of them, of different genders and ethnic backgrounds, gay and straight, completely naked but draped in sheer, silver silk capes. They formed two orderly queues. One queue led towards Santa and displayed a sign 'naughty' the other led to a wooden horse displaying 'good'. Still looking through the keyhole, I sighed, and rubbed my eyes. *Could this really be happening?*

Absolutely intrigued, I cautiously entered the room and was beckoned by one of Santa's drag queens to put on a silver cape. I was also handed a magnificent blue *velluto* mask to wear. I removed my clothes and stepped into my cape behind a vintage green and gold, dressing screen. I then placed the mask on my face, before being sprayed with an exquisite parfum. After all, we all need to smell good in order to accentuate our glamorous, feminine side.

As the queue headed towards Santa, I observed that, one by one, the adults dropped their capes, to reveal their naked bodies. In turn, they then lay across his legs and Santa spanked them with his candy cane, making them feel sexually needy. They were the 'naughty' ones; those who had been disobedient. The others proceeded towards the wooden horse. These were the 'good' ones.

As they each lined up in their appropriate lines, caped and ready, they were given shots of red wine infused with blue lotus extract. They each wore exquisite and beautiful masks, some more stunning than others, but all were extremely flamboyant.

One by one, the good ones sat upon the horse, lining up their self-impression, their own individual gender and need. Their imprint of their erogenous zones hovered over a hole in the centre of the horse, where a saddle would sit. It was like a helicopter waiting to land. The horse started to move up and down, and from side to side, as the North Pole rocket vibrator revealed itself, rising from the horse's saddle ready to make its grand tour of your chosen entrance to excite, tease and satisfy your requirements.

The North Pole vibrator was large, wide, and had the appearance of a big icicle. It appeared glass-like but was able to quickly switch temperatures, between cold and warm. It was just enough to excite, arouse and satisfy. A bit like putting anti-freeze into a car engine to stop it seizing up. 'If you don't use it, you lose it, baby.' For added pleasure, you could adjust its size and shape from the reins in front.

Icicles suddenly dripped down the sides making the thrill delightfully pleasurable, as it speeded up then down.

There were stirrups on either side that you could push down on, allowing yourself to raise and heighten your position as the vibrator penetrated for deeper satisfaction.

Santa asked if I had been good. My nod to him indicated that I had. Did that mean I too, could collect my ticket to ride his North Pole rocket?

Wouldn't you want to ride the rocket, or would you prefer a spank with a candy cane? Maybe both would be perfect in adult, fantasy realms. I wonder if Mrs Claus gets spanked and the elves get to ride. Elf on the shelf? More like the elf, helping himself to some blue lotus.

Did you know (Blue Lotus)

The blue lotus, not to be confused with the blue lily, was popular in ancient Egypt, where it was known as the party drug. A powerful aphrodisiac, it led to sexually-themed orgies.

When Tutankhamun's body was uncasked in 1922, it was discovered to have been scattered with blue lotus flowers and, within the tomb, was found 'the lotus chalice'. The blue lotus flower is used for meditation and massage and symbolises tranquillity and peace. It has an extraordinarily strong fragrance and was used by the Egyptians for many perfumes. It was, and is, a transformational essence, spiritual and calming, and aids in lucid dreaming. The blue lotus contains psychoactive alkaloid aporphines.

The blue lotus (*nelumbo nucifera*) was known to the Mayans as well as the Egyptians.

It has been used for thousands of years and its effects range from sedative, euphoria (the feel-good feeling), mild hallucinations, and sexual stimulation. Maybe that is what is going on in the Turin Papyrus of Egypt? It seems the Turin Papyrus suggests orgies.

Blue lotus is illegal for human consumption in many counties now but may be found as an oil or incense. It lives 'beneath the surface' in muddy ponds and streams and then appears at sunrise, venturing on top of the water and the blossoms open. In the evening, it then closes and pops back down, securing itself into the mud. When the sun rises the next day, it proceeds, once again, to the top of the water to open and show the world its splendour! It's like the fountain of life, simply beautiful. ('Fountain of Life', Incognito, *Beneath the Surface*, 1996.)

Chapter 9

Santa's farewell gifts

After the conference (more of that later), I re-entered my bedroom, walked towards the Christmas tree, and removed a red love heart from the tree. It made me feel sad and alone, without anyone special in my life. If only I could find 'Mr Right'. Does 'Mr Right' even exist? Were my expectations too high? Santa once again appeared and walked towards my bed and reached inside his magical sack (the red cloth one, of course). He pulled out a box and laid it on the reindeer skin, before walking back towards the door.

Then he turned, looked at me, grinned, and said, 'So, you experienced my morphs on your flight and landing yesterday. I acted dumb, and responded, 'Morphs, what morphs?'

'My dear, I don't only have elves on my shelf.' Santa chuckled, holding on to his large stomach. 'So, let me allow your adult fantasies to always be there for you when you need them, take my morphed men. Take them from your selection box of 'Fancy That!' and taste them, savour them, and enjoy yourself. If that doesn't give you pleasure, there is a bonus; my 'North Pole rocket vibrator' which can be naughty or nice, but you will need a ticket to ride. Your life will never again be the same. What else are women's dreams made of? Chocolate!'

My chocolate box of Morphs

Santa had gone one step further, from fantasising morphs of dough to chocolate temptation. The box he had left on my bed was real. He had given me a beautiful selection box of morphing men and coated them in chocolate. He named the box 'Fancy That!'

Mr Lover – 90% dark chocolate
Mr DIY – milk chocolate
Mr Funny – white and milk chocolate popping candy nuts
Mr Latino – lime crunch
Mr Spa – smooth white chocolate with peppermint bubbles
Mr Good-Looking – creamy fudge dream
Mr Rich – golden caramel
Mr Overseas – salted cruise toffee
Mr Michelin Chef – chilli and ginger

And Santa even threw in a couple of special editions:

'Pussy Wink Surprise' – pina colada liquor
'Nymphy Handshake' – Baileys and rum

So, the next time one of my girlfriends is feeling low, going through a divorce, needing a specific man, or feeling burnt out, I will take her a box of 'Fancy That!'. I might even grab one for myself.

A bottle of wine, some fantasy, philosophy, humour, sex, and a box of 'Fancy That!', isn't that exactly what's needed when your girlfriend comes to visit you feeling depressed and, more importantly, in need of fun and a taste of chocolate.

Santa certainly boxed me up a variety of men! Although I never got to meet the last three, I wonder if I ever will.

- Mr Rich
- Mr Overseas
- Mr Michelin Chef

For now, I am sure looking forward to tasting them!
('Mr Right', Leona Lewis, *Christmas with Love*, 2013.)

Did you know (chocolate)

Chocolate is a medicine. The Ancient Mayans and Aztecs used it for spiritual and ceremonial purposes.

Cacao is the seed that chocolate is made from. It is raw and has not been processed, while cocoa is an ingredient that has been processed to make chocolate bars. The purest form of chocolate is raw cacao (pronounced ka cow). It is a potent superfood. Pretty cool, hey. No wonder so many women love chocolate. It can improve your mood and contains L-arginine, an amino acid that can be an effective sex-enhancer. Dark chocolate is healthier than milk or white chocolate but hey, who cares? It's irresistible, tempting and oh so naughty. ('Chocolates', Kevin Aviance, *Box of Chocolates*, 1999.)

If you are interested in reading my spiritual philosophy from when I chaired the conference at the ice hotel, please continue to the next chapter and you may find something that will resonate with you.

Thank you for being a part of my book; a reflection of everyday life, a bit of fancy that!

It's great to have the real deal in a relationship, ready to perform and light up your many desires, ready to spruce up your love life. However, if all else fails, take a moment to do some pussy winking, and certainly indulge in a box of 'Fancy That!' After all, a little bit of what you fancy, does you good ladies, wink! Which guy would you choose to go on a date with and savour in your mouth? Whichever morph you select, you will be the girl of his dreams.

Maybe if I ask Santa, he could magically transform all my morphs again, and place them around my ice bed, laden with reindeer skin. They could all serenade me with 'Luck be a Lady Tonight', wink! ('Luck be a Lady Tonight', Frank Sinatra, *My Kind of Broadway*, 1965.)

Chapter 10

The conference

Spiritual philosophy

With anxiety racing through my body and a slight shaking of hands, I grabbed my notes and started my speech. In all fairness, I couldn't see Santa in the audience, but I was certain he was there, observing me.

Welcome Friends!

I know many of you have travelled a long way and I hope you are rested from the long trip.

I would like to start with the spiritual, mystical island of Es Vedra, Ibiza. It is extremely famous. It appeared as 'Bali Hai' the volcanic rock in the 1958 Hollywood smash hit movie South Pacific.

Legend reveals that after the North Pole and Bermuda Triangle, Es Vedra is the third most magnetic spot-on earth. According to popular myth, Es Vedra was the home of the sirens and sea-nymphs. (Maybe that is where Nymphy came from? Was she trying to capture magnetic energy to take back to Es Vedra from the North Pole, or was she really from Petra?) It seems people are drawn to Es Vedra because of the mysterious force people feel around the area. It is a favourite place for meditation and other spiritual practices. UFOs have also been seen and strange circles of light orbing the sea around the island. It is uninhabited by humans, and only lizards and goats live there.

Maybe Es Vedra is there to educate us in spirit and earth energy and show us how powerful spirit is. From meditation to spiritualism, we are moving into a more spiritual era, a time to open our hearts and start to use our insight, our intuition, and gut feelings. "Why?" you might ask. Because our spirit, our soul, is real and never really dies. Our bodies are just a shell that covers our soul and we, in turn, get into character, good or bad. We have our script and off we go until it's time to return home, back to our spirit land.

So, when you feel that feeling from Es Vedra; the feeling of peace, love, and security, is that not the feeling of heaven, our spiritual home full of love? That's why when we experience such a feeling, it draws us in. You remember and your spirit can resonate on a higher vibration of energy. That is the reason we love music; something within our chemistry warms to certain tones and vibrations, the pitch and sound makes us happy or can produce tears and bring out emotions. The frequency of music is the speed of the vibrations! Maybe you should try a gong bath or a singing bowl meditation, you may be surprised at how your body will interact! Give it a go, "nothing ventured, nothing gained".

('Take Me To This Place', Camiel, *Café Del Mar*, 2019.)

Our Spirit Garden: lessons to be learned on Earth

As we move into a more spiritual existence, we need to awaken and look after our planet. Climate change is a real threat that needs to be addressed. We will not be able to enjoy everything life has to offer if we have no planet on which to live.

Air is essential for our survival and so is water. Our body is made up of 95% water and is sacred to existence. If we have no trees, no air, no water, no food, only floods, storms, and contaminated food, we have nothing. We can no longer swing on a beautiful hammock on a beautiful desert island, or walk hand in hand on golden sands on that beach, because it will no longer exist.

The conference

*A reminder from the spirit how precious earth is, as Floyd Westerman, 'Red Crow' the 'Kanghi Duta' of the Sioux Indians (1936–2007), once said, **'Our DNA is the same as the trees. A tree breathes what we exhale, when the tree exhales, we need to breathe what the tree has exhaled.'** Super cool quote, hey!* ('The Memory of Trees', Enya, *The Memory of Trees*, 1995.)

Everything has a spirit, and we need to live on earth in a spiritual, loving way. We need to plant something to connect with Mother Earth. For all those gardeners out there, you may recognise the uplifting feeling when your troubles seem to disappear while working in the garden, or planting seeds/flowers in your window boxes. You get the same feeling walking through a forest, that connection with the earth. If you have never experienced it, maybe you should give it a go. Take a walk in the forest, plant bulbs, smell the roses, mow the lawn, or visit a country garden. Whatever you decide, breathe in the air, connect with spirit, and feel your mood change, shift and lift.

Some people are so stressed out that they drive from A to B and then wonder how they got there as they weren't concentrating. If you connect spirit with nature, you may well question how you cut down the bushes, mowed the lawn, planted the seeds, or walked through the forest. You will have soaked in pure love from the earth without realising two hours have passed, and you have forgotten that bill you need to pay, that court case you have been pulled into or the fear you have of flying.

My dear, departed mum, had a plaque in her garden. It read: 'The kiss of the sun for pardon, the song of the bird for mirth. One is nearer to God in a garden than anywhere else on earth'.

Ask yourself who you are, what is the true meaning of your existence here on earth before you return home to spirit. When you die, what experience or knowledge will you take back with you? Maybe you don't care, but perhaps you should.

The conference

You must learn and attain wisdom from your experiences of life. How will others learn if you don't share your wisdom? Go backpacking in Tibet, watch the sunset in Marrakech, sign up for that knitting class, play with the kids and leave the housework to another day; go shopping for an elderly neighbour, talk to that stranger you feel connected to, write that book, produce that song, fly a plane, or simply sit in a garden and meditate. Live your life, respect, love, learn, offer your knowledge, be kind, venture into the garden, trust your intuition and open your spiritual eye. Most of all, laugh, smile, and listen to uplifting music that gives your spirit frisson and lifts your vibrations.

Hug a tree and breathe. You may be pleasantly surprised. Spirit is real, it's all around each one of us. I am not suggesting you dance around a tree naked in the woods, just reconnect with nature; feel its presence and the calm feeling it produces. We may still be able to save our planet from destruction.

Love is pure; love is what we all need and desire. It doesn't matter what your religious views are, what matters is to enjoy your spiritual path - the spirit you were born with, the spirit that lives inside your shell, your body, and the same spirit which will return home one day to the great creator of our galaxy. We will return to the spirit world.

The Celestine Prophecy by James Redfield, 1993, describes energy fields. We are energy, we are love. Mother Earth needs peace, respect and for our planet to be appreciated. We must acknowledge our beautiful oceans, blue skies, flowers, animals, our moon, our sun, and our stars – but how many do you notice? Have a look; you may like what you have been missing, or have been too busy to appreciate.

We are so into our ego, our wanting, our taking, jealousy, anger, drugs and destruction, we have lost respect for what is free. Planet Earth and all the beauty it holds and gives us. Our new spiritual awaking is on its way; our energy will change; it must bring world peace, stop cruelty and racism. We are from one spirit and each one of us is connected to the other.

Something else to think about!

Is someone entering your life or are you entering theirs? They appear or you do, at just the right time, to assist with that difficulty. Their expert guidance supports you or you support them. They will aid you emotionally and spiritually and be your physical wall to support you.

They will feel like your guardian angel and, of course, they are. They have appeared and manifested to help you. They will say or act in a way to bring that relationship to an end. 'What relationship?' you may ask. The relationship that is pulling you down, the reason you can't sleep at night. This could be a romantic one, a work or family relationship that is causing you great concern. They may walk away or leave you from their own departure, death. They may even, through their actions, force you to take a stand, speak up or defend yourself. We must understand that, through their actions, our needs have been met. We have had our desires fulfilled and there is no work left for them to do, so they leave us. They have an affair, they die, they disappear, they move away or simply break up from you and move on. You may cry, you may miss them or feel relief that they have departed. However, they may return later in your life, very unexpectedly. Having unfinished business, they reappear in your life.

Why? Because you sent up a prayer and it was answered. Your time to move on and take what you have learned is precious.

Lifetime relationships can teach lifetime lessons. You may not like them but without them, how else will you grow and learn? To have a solid emotional foundation you must love the person or at least respect the part of them that has led you on to your path today. Remember, if you never experienced something, good or bad, or you had not met them you would not have been placed on your new path. Sometimes we must suffer something to appreciate the outcome.

- *If that bitch from the office hadn't been so mean to you, you would still be there and would have missed your chance to move to a new company that appreciates your qualities and allowed you to grow.*
- *If your narcissistic ex-husband hadn't run off with the neighbour, you would still be constrained and not allowed to spread your wings, grow, and be appreciated. From the tears he made you suffer, sunrise has now emerged. You are a stronger person. You are thankful for being put through hell. His day is yet to come from his own learnings and the neighbour may now encounter what you once experienced - narcissistic behaviour.*
- *The ex-wife was so taken up with her horses, she had no time for her husband.*

He has since moved to Australia and now owns his own stables. He has met a woman who rides with him, emotionally and sexually. His ex-wife now wants him back.

Don't you just love Karma? You must use what you learn and put it to good use in all relationships and areas of your life. Can you see what lessons were learned? Both men and women are equally guilty. We all should learn and be responsible for our actions, what we create and how we hurt others in our quest for control. After all, we are just characters in one large world book, all having a screen part to play. Once played out, we learn from playing our part and return back to spirit, one thinks!

Psychic sex, Telepathy: awakening our sexual spiritual mind

We are born, we grow, we become adults and we desire sex.

The conference

It does not matter what our beliefs are, what religion we have chosen, what food we prefer, what car we drive or what language we speak. It boils down to one thing; we all have that urge, that feeling, that desire for sex.

- *We have emotions.*
- *We have feelings.*
- *We cry.*
- *We laugh.*

But we all want sex - well, most of us do.

To take sex to another level and, to be honest, is there anything above tantric sex? Well, yes, possibly there is, maybe it's 'psychic sex' or "telepathic sex". It sounds paranormal but could be exquisite. Although this is not medically proven, you can experience this in your mind.

Maybe it's not psychic or telepathic sex; maybe it's just plain MIND SEX!

There is no need for Viagra or sex toys. Mind sex is a form of meditation but far easier to achieve and attain. Anyone can try this.

While sitting or lying down in a quiet place where you will not be disturbed, close your eyes and take deep breaths in and out. Drop your shoulders and continue breathing deeply until you feel calm and relaxed. Think of someone you like. This could be your partner, old flame, work colleague, or even a celebrity,

Within your mind, look at their face and how they are dressed. Imagine if they smell good. Do they have a distinctive odour about them or are they wearing a sensual perfume or aftershave?

Picture the scene, where are you both? At a movie, in a car, in bed or even in a park? Is it daytime or night-time? What is the temperature? Is it cold or hot? Are you on a beach and your bodies are silky, wet or slimy from suntan lotion? Is there music playing? If so, is it loud, sensual, meditative chanting or are there birds singing? Have you both shared a meal? Can you smell garlic on your partner's lips? Have you drunk wine together or shared some whipped cream?

Once you have visualised the setting, touch them with your mind's eye. Touch their fingers, their face, their hands, their chest, their legs, and lower extremities. Activate all your senses at once.

Kiss them, hold them, and imagine them touching you back, reciprocating your caresses. Now continue until you reach orgasm. Try it, you may amaze yourself. Enough said. Wink!

So, when we leave our earthly body, do we still have or require sex? Who knows? Sex would be on a completely different frequency, one thinks! I feel mind/telepathic sex is our future, especially when we all turn into robots and our bodies are replaced by machines. Maybe our mind, psychic telepathy is drawn towards a 'Psychedelic Love'.

('Psychedelic Love', Natalie Williams, *Secret Garden*, 2006.)

I hope my words resonated with you and each one of you will reflect on my philosophy. And remember, if you can't go another day without someone, tell them. They just may be the one, or it may be just what they need to hear. To love someone, may mean loving in a million ways. Who knows where it can lead to, or the happiness it can bring someone! After all, we all want to be loved, yes? ('A Million Ways', Tony Momrelle, *Keep Pushing*, 2015.)

Applause!

www.ingramcontent.com/pod-product-compliance
Lightning Source LLC
Chambersburg PA
CBHW021106080526
44587CB00010B/407